CONTENT

CORE BADGES

BE PREPARED...

Core badges

Taking part and being an active member of your
Scout Troop is something to be proud of. That's
why there are badges you can earn as you go.

Staged activity badges 129

SCOUTS: HERE'S WHERE THE FUN BEGINS

There are so many possibilities to try new skills, new experiences and new challenges as a Scout. There are lots of activity badges. You might even decide to improve your skills through the staged activity badges. And if you really want to make the most of your time as a Scout, you could go for the ultimate – the Chief Scout's Gold Award.

Anything's possible. And all the details of the Scout badges and awards are in this book.

Whatever challenge you decide to try, your Scout leader and other adults can help you. That's why we've divided this book into two sections:

- The first part is for you to read. We hope it's easy to understand. If anything's not clear, or there's a word you're not familiar with, ask your leader or another adult.
- The second part has a few notes for any adult helping you earn your badges or awards. It will help them to support you through each challenge.

Which badges will you choose?

When you're deciding which badges you would like to work towards, think about whether it meets your needs, interests, and skill level. So if you're going for something like a staged activity badge, think about doing the stage that best matches your abilities and experience, rather than your age. Any activity should stretch you a little.

You should be involved as much as possible in choosing which badges you work towards, as part of your participation on the programme planning. You can find out more about how can shape Scouting at **scouts.org.uk/youthinvolvement**

Not sure if you're able to do what's needed for a badge? Don't worry!

If there's a badge in this book that you'd really like to try, but you're not sure you can do what we're asking for, have a chat with your Scout leader. They are able to change the things you have to do to earn a badge, depending on your abilities.

It would be a shame if you couldn't try something you really liked, because something was getting in your way. So long as the activity is still challenging enough for you, there will always be a way your leader can help you take part.

Badges can even be tailored to make them more difficult, if what's in this book is too easy. You can also gain the Activity Plus badge for most activities if you need more of a challenge. And if you're able to pass your skills onto others, you could even go for the Instructor badge.

 If you see this symbol on the page, it means your Leader will need to follow specific rules to make sure you're safe.

So when you're thinking about your next activity, make sure you look though this book together with your leader or another adult who is helping you.

MEMBERSHIP AWARD

This award is about helping you to understand the commitment you are making when you make your Promise and become a Scout. It is presented at your Investiture ceremony.

How to earn your badge

1. Know about the Scout Troop:
   - Get to know other members and Leaders in the Patrol and Troop.
   - Find out about the ceremonies and traditions in the Troop.
   - Find out about the activities that the Patrol and Troop does.
2. Know about joining your Troop:
   - Learn and understand the Scout Promise and Law and the rules of the Troop.
   - Learn and understand the Scout Motto, sign, salute and handshake.
   - Show you know the general history and family of Scouts and Scouting around the world.
   - Learn what to do at Investiture.
3. Become a Scout by making the Promise.

JOINING IN AWARD

These badges celebrate your commitment and participation in Scouting.

How to earn your badges
The badges are numbered, and you can be awarded a new badge every 12 months from the time you joined Scouting. If you were a member in a previous section, the badge numbers will continue from the ones you have already been awarded.

You collect these badges throughout your time in Beavers, Cubs, Scouts and Explorers. They recognise how long you have been a member of the Scout movement in total. You can earn up to four of these badges while you're a Scout.

MOVING ON AWARD (SCOUTS TO EXPLORERS)

This badge marks the point when you leave your Scout Troop to join an Explorer Unit.

How to earn your badge
1. Find out what your options are for being an Explorer in your area. This includes finding out about the Young Leaders' Scheme.
2. Attend both Scouts and Explorers for a short period of time (at least three weeks). Take an active part in the Explorer Unit programme.

You can work for the Explorer Membership Award while you earn your Moving on Award.

LEADERSHIP STRIPES

A Scout Troop is usually organised into smaller groups called Patrols, each headed up by a Patrol Leader, and often with an Assistant Patrol Leader and Senior Patrol Leader as well. Senior Patrol Leader, Patrol Leaders and Assistant Patrol Leaders wear leadership stripes to recognise their roles.

CORE BADGES

ACTIVITY BADGES

BE ADVENTUROUS...

Activity badges

There are so many different topics and subjects to try through activity badges. They give you the chance to reach a goal in something you're interested in. You'll probably do them when you're at Troop meetings.

So go ahead. Try something new, learn a skill and achieve your goals.

ACTIVITY CENTRE SERVICE

Scout Activity Centres are really important places in Scouting. By completing this badge, you can help to look after them. You'll be making sure that other Scouts are able to enjoy them while looking after the surrounding environment.

How to earn your badge

1. Help the warden or manager and work for at least five days at a permanent District, County or National Scout campsite. Alternatively, you can do this work at a similar activity centre.

2. Explain and show how to use three items of equipment that you've used in your work with the activity centre. Show or talk about how you maintain the equipment.

3. Choose four of these to explain and if possible demonstrate:
   - the use of computers in campsite management
   - how to take care of campers' needs while respecting wildlife
   - how to prevent frozen pipes and what to do if an overground pipe bursts or leaks
   - the need for good site drainage and clear ditches

- rubbish disposal and how to recycle materials wherever possible
- the reasons for having clean toilets
- how to unblock a drain
- how to use and maintain equipment for an activity you have become familiar with
- other important tasks that the warden or manager has pointed out.

4. Talk about developments and improvements you would like to see at a permanent campsite. It could be the one you worked at or another one you know well.

AIR OR SEA NAVIGATION

Be the one who knows the way to go – at sea or by air. Learn a skill that would help you navigate your crew on your journey.

How to earn your badge
Choose one of these options. Then complete all of the tasks under the option you've chosen.

Option 1: air
1. Using simple diagrams, illustrate latitude and longitude.
2. Using a compass, show how an aircraft can be turned on to various compass headings.
3. Show that you understand how a compass works, including the difference between magnetic, true and grid north.
4. Explain what magnetic deviation is and how it applies to air navigation.
5. Show that you know about the latest developments in electronic navigation aids.
6. You'll be given three headings and corresponding tracks. For each one, work out the amount of drift in degrees and the type. Show your answers by drawing a simple diagram.

7. Complete one of these:
   - On a topographical air map, draw a track for an imaginary flight of at least 80 nautical miles. Point out the landmarks that would show up on both sides of the track, in clear visibility, at an altitude of about 600 feet.
   - Identify landmarks on a topographical air map that you would see during a flight of about half an hour in clear weather.

8. On a topographical map, draw the track between any two places at least 100 nautical miles apart. Measure the exact distance.

9. Show that you can calculate overhead flight times, using the air speed of an aircraft, and adjust your calculations for head and tail winds of different speeds.

If the aircraft's air speed is 130 knots, what would be the time of flight from overhead starting point to overhead destination? Work this out for each of these conditions:
   - with no wind at all
   - with a head wind of 30 knots
   - with a tail wind of 50 knots.

Option 2: sea

1. Gain a good working knowledge of charts, chart datum and symbols used.
2. Show your skills in compass work by completing all of these tasks:
   - Read a mariner's compass marked in points and degrees and demonstrate your knowledge of compasses generally.
   - Show that you know about variation and avoiding deviation.
   - Show you're able to correct a magnetic compass course for variation and deviation to obtain a true bearing. Next, adjust a given true bearing to obtain a compass course.
   - Show how compass error can be found from a transit bearing.
3. Complete two of these tasks:
   - Show how a position can be found from two intersecting position lines.
   - Learn what is meant by a 'cocked hat' position and how to use it safely. Plot a position from any three cross bearings.
   - Plot a position using the 'running fix' method.
   - Plot a position using a combination of compass bearings and one or more of these: satellite navigation system, vertical sextant angle, horizontal sextant angle, line of sounding or transits.
4. Learn how to use tide tables and tidal stream atlases.

5. Learn how to use the marine log to obtain distance run and speed.
6. Show you understand the buoyage system for United Kingdom coastal waters and other methods of marking dangers and channels.
7. Show that you're aware of the latest developments in electronic technology, like the Global Positioning System and electronic charts.
8. Go on a coastal voyage of between four and six hours and act as the navigator. You should keep a log showing courses steered, distance run, navigation marks passed and weather experienced. During the voyage:
   - plot the estimated position every hour by keeping up the dead reckoning
   - at least once per hour, and whenever appropriate, plot an observed position by bearings or other means of obtaining a fix.

AIR RESEARCHER

Find out more about one of humanity's greatest accomplishments – developing the technology to fly through the air.

Here's what you need to do to earn this badge.

1. Research one historical aspect of flight, and share what you find out with the Troop. You might like to find out about:
   - the development of aviation or flight over a period of time agreed with your leader
   - balloons or airships, from their first appearance to the present day
   - a type of aero engine, such as a jet or piston engines in general, or a specific engine like the Rolls Royce Merlin
   - the development of an aircraft type, like a Spitfire, Boeing 747, Harrier, Stealth Bomber, space shuttle or the Wessex helicopter. You could find out details about its history, role and achievements.

2. While you're doing your research, visit at least one place of interest that relates to your chosen subject. It could be a museum, an air display or an aeronautics factory.

3. Present what you have found out.
Your presentation should include a model that
you have made based on your subject. You
should also include diagrams and pictures
wherever you can.

If you're visiting an airfield be sure to know
the Scouting rules. Your leader can find these
at **scouts.org.uk/por**

AIR SPOTTER

Can you tell an Airbus from a Boeing. Take up your binoculars, look to the skies and go for the Air Spotter activity badge.

How to earn your badge
1. Learn to recognise, by sight, 38 out of the 50 aircraft listed in The Scout Association's Aircraft Recognition List.
2. Complete one of these activities:
   • By yourself or with another Scout, take photographs or collect pictures of at least 10 different aircraft types. Name the different types and their uses.
   • Keep a log of aircraft you've spotted over at least four weeks. Note down dates and times, the aircraft you saw and distinctive features you can recognise them by. Also note the aircraft's approximate heading.
3. Complete one of these activities:
   • Recognise and name the national aircraft markings, both service and civil, of at least six countries including the United Kingdom.
   • Learn the RAF and NATO system of letter designation according to aircraft function. Give examples of three designations.

- Name three basic training aircraft used in private flying. Give a brief report on one, naming a club and airfield where it is used. Try to make it a local airfield, if possible.

4. Describe the main features you would use to recognise six aircraft, which have been chosen by an appropriate adult.

ANGLER

If you'd love to know how to reel in a big catch, or just develop a hobby where you can enjoy the water, why not go for the Angler activity badge?

How to earn your badge

If you have The Angling Trust Cast Level Two award, you can automatically qualify for the Angler badge. If not, here's what you need to do to earn this badge.

1. Learn the water safety rules and the proper precautions to take when fishing from the bank, shore line, or from a boat.
2. Learn the basic hygiene precautions to take when fishing.
3. Go fishing at least four times in two different places. Make a note of:
   - the number of fish you caught
   - species and size of your fish
   - your method, tackle and bait used
   - the weather and water conditions.
4. Choose the correct equipment and method for where you plan to fish.
5. Learn to assemble a rod, reel or pole.
6. Choose the right form of bait, lure or fly for your planned fishing activity.

7. Show you can cast correctly and accurately into a target area a suitable distance away, depending on the equipment you are using.
8. Tie at least three different knots for your chosen method of fishing.
9. Show how to correctly handle a fish, unhook it and return it into the water.
10. Explain how different species of fish have different habitats. Talk about how this, and weather conditions, can affect your method of fishing.

❗ If you're 13 or older, you'll need a rod license to fish salmon, trout, freshwater fish, smelt and eels with a rod and line in England, Wales or the Border Esk region of Scotland. Find out more on the UK Government website at **gov.uk/fishing-licences**

Top tips
Number 7 mentions casting from a 'suitable distance'. Here's what we mean:
- If you're using beach fishing tackle, cast from 45 metres.
- For a ledger and float tackle, cast into a 1-metre circle at least three times out of six, at a distance of 9 metres.
- For a trout fly on a fly line, cast into a 3-metre circle at least three times out of eight, at a distance of 11 metres.

ARTIST

Art is really interesting – it stretches your imagination, makes you think and helps you to express yourself. Whether you create art or just appreciate it, take the artist badge and show what you've learned.

How to earn your badge
Choose from Options 1 or 2. Then complete all tasks under your chosen option.

Option 1: artist
1. Paint, draw or illustrate each of these:
    - a scene from a story
    - a person or object
    - a landscape.
2. Show a selection of your own recent work.

Option 2: arts enthusiast
1. Choose a favourite art form or artist to take an active interest in. It doesn't have to be painting – it could be pop music, sculpture, theatre, architecture, break dancing or anything similar.
2. Describe two visits you have made that are connected to your interest. You can use photographs, films, recordings, concert programmes, ticket stubs, newspaper reviews or websites to illustrate your point.

3. Show that you know a lot about an aspect of your interest. You could talk about a particular piece of art, like a painting, performance, sculpture or building. Or you could discuss a particular person or historical period connected with your chosen art form.
4. Make a list of major events, exhibitions or venues connected with your chosen subject. Talk about why the items on your list are important.

ASTRONAUTICS

A smart man called Carl Sagan once said, "Somewhere, something incredible is waiting to be known," Start your journey of space exploration here, and who knows? Something incredible could be waiting for you.

How to earn your badge

1. Find out how craters are formed, and what meteorites tell us about the universe. You could experiment using marbles, rubber balls or stones as meteorites, and a tray filled with sand as your planet/moon surface.

2. Compare satellite images of Mars and the moon with satellite images of Earth. Point out similar landscape features such as craters, valleys and volcanoes. Discuss what Earth observation can tell us about the land, sea and atmosphere.

3. Build your own satellite dish. Cover a torch in paper slits and a range of mirrors, flat and concave, to show how concave satellite dishes focus signals from satellites. Discuss what everyday items rely on satellites.

4. In a group, debate about life elsewhere in the universe. What might it look like? How do we search for life on other planets and moons? How would the human race react to the discovery of life elsewhere in the universe?
5. Find out about the International Space Station and how astronauts live and work on board.
6. Research a current space mission, such as a mission to Mars. Then, design a model of your own space probe or other spacecraft, including the instruments on board that enable it to complete its mission.
7. Build, launch and recover a model rocket. Think about the shape of your rocket and why that's important. Make a second launch to achieve a specific objective, such as reaching a certain height or carrying a fragile payload, like an egg.

ASTRONOMER

Would you like to navigate the night sky, from the Big Dipper to Orion's Belt? Take up your telescope and become an astronomer.

How to earn your badge

1. Show what you know about the night sky and why the pattern of stars changes, night by night, throughout the year.
2. Learn the meaning of the terms celestial, equator, poles, circumpolar and zodiac.
3. Build a model of the solar system using everyday materials found in the home, such as different size fruit or sports balls. Use an outside area to scale the solar system.
4. Explain how the Moon affects the tides.
5. Build a telescope from two cardboard tubes or two A4 pieces of black card and lenses. Compare what you can see through a telescope and what you can see with the naked eye.
6. Observe three constellations on a clear night and record what you saw.
7. Read a star map using a compass and red light. Compare the differences between using a star map and a normal map.

8. Learn how to identify a satellite. How do you tell it apart from an aeroplane, star, planet or a meteor? Then complete these activities:
a. identify a satellite to observe
b. choose a clear night and use a clock and a compass to help you observe the satellite
c. plan an evening with your Scout Group and teach others how to observe the satellite.

Top tips
For number 5, you will need these materials to make your telescope: corrugated cardboard, sticky tape, scissors, a pair of compasses or a pencil and ruler, two glass or plastic lenses of different sizes (like two magnifying glasses). Both lenses must be smaller in diameter than the cardboard tubes you make.

For useful information about stargazing visit **http://tinyurl.com/jcjjt3z**

ATHLETICS

If you're inspired by our Olympic heroes, why not work on your personal best? Athletics is all about practising, persevering and improving – perfect for a Scout like you. You earn the Athletics badge for taking part and putting in your best effort, so have a go and give it your best shot.

Here's what you need to do to earn this badge.
1. Run through an appropriate warm-up and warm-down routine using all the main muscle groups. Explain why both routines are important.
2. Talk about the safety rules in athletics, particularly throwing and jumping events. Explain the most appropriate clothing to wear.
3. Take part in six athletics events. Choose at least one from each of the three sections below, improving your distance or time over a number of attempts.

Field events	Track events	Team events
Discus	100m	4 x100m relay
Shot put	200m	Team
Throwing a	400m	assault course
cricket ball	800m	Assisted
Javelin	1500m	blindfold race
High jump	100m hurdles	
Long jump		
Standing jump		
Sargent jump		

4. Find out and explain to your leader how to take part in athletics in your local area.

Top tips
- For number 1 you might decide to do skipping, running on the spot, stretching both arms high above your head and then relaxing down, bending the knees and dropping the head or rolling the head slowly around, tensing and relaxing the shoulders.
- For the field events, we recommend the shot weighs around 2.73kg, the discus 1kg and the cricket ball 0.135kg.

You must be especially careful when doing the high jump. You'll need to think about the way you're going to jump, how you're going to land and what you're going to land on! You must use the proper equipment and, unless expert tuition and supervision is available, you must not attempt the Fosbury Flop. The scissor jump is an easier way to do it.

ATHLETICS PLUS

The name says it all – improve on what you've learned through the Athletics badge and reach new targets.

Before you attempt Athletics Plus, you must hold the Athletics activity badge.

Here's what you need to do to earn this badge.
1. Run through an appropriate warm up and warm down routine using all the main muscle groups. Explain why both routines are important.
2. Talk about the safety rules for athletics, particularly throwing and jumping events.
3. Compete in any three events (two track and one field, or vice versa) and gain the points set out as indicated on the score chart below.

Points	Distance				
	100m sprint sec	200m sprint sec	400m sec	800m min	1500m min
10	13.4	28.0	64.0	2.30	5.10
9	14.0	28.8	67.0	2.40	5.25
8	14.7	31.4	71.0	3.00	5.45
7	15.3	32.6	75.0	3.10	5.50
6	15.8	33.2	79.0	3.20	6.20
5	16.3	34.0	83.0	3.40	6.50
4	16.8	35.5	88.0	4.00	7.30
3	17.6	38.3	94.0	4.20	8.00
2	18.3	40.0	100.0	4.40	8.30
1	20.0	45.0	120.0	5.00	9.30

Points	High Jump Mtr	Long Jump Mtr	Shot Mtr	Discus Mtr	Cricket Ball Mtr
10	1.60	5.00	9.5	35.0	65.0
9	1.40	4.75	8.5	29.0	55.0
8	1.30	4.40	7.2	22.0	50.0
7	1.25	4.20	6.5	17.0	45.0
6	1.20	4.00	5.5	14.0	35.0
5	1.00	3.75	4.1	12.0	30.0
4	0.90	3.30	3.7	10.0	25.0
3	0.85	2.80	3.3	9.0	20.0
2	0.80	2.45	2.8	8.5	15.0
1	0.75	2.10	1.8	6.0	10.0

Minimum points total for the award of badge	
Age	Points
Under 11	6
Under 12	9
Under 13	13
Under 14	17
Under 15	22

Top tips

- Ideally you should work towards this badge as part of a Scout activity. If that's not possible, you may use timings or distances you've achieved at school or other athletic events. A teacher or athletics coach can confirm your timings.
- For the field events, we recommended the shot weighs around 2.73kg, the discus 1kg and the cricket ball 0.135kg.

You must be especially careful when doing the high jump. You'll need to think about the way you're going to jump, how you're going to land and what you're going to land on! You must use the proper equipment at all times and, unless expert tuition and supervision is available, you must not attempt the Fosbury Flop. The scissor jump is an easier way to do it.

CAMPER

Show you have the knowledge
and skills to go on a camping
adventure. This isn't just about
taking part in a camping trip –

this activity tests your ability to prepare everything
you need for a night sleeping under the stars.

How to earn your badge

1. Camp under canvas as a Scout for at least
   15 nights.
2. Lead a group of Scouts in the pitching, striking
   and packing of a four to six person tent.
3. Find out what to look for when choosing a
   campsite and in deciding the best position to
   pitch tents.
4. Show that you understand and act on the
   reasons for hygiene and the importance of
   being safe and tidy in camp.
5. Show how you store food hygienically at camp.
6. Learn how to dispose of your rubbish safely
   and responsibly.
7. Construct two useful camp gadgets, such as a
   camp larder, altar fire, flagpole or a camp gate.
8. Plan a full menu for a weekend camp. Cook a
   full meal from it over an open fire.
9. With others in your Troop, plan and carry out a
   programme of activities for a weekend camp.

Top tips
When we say 'under canvas', we mean any kind of tent, bivouac or natural shelter.

CAVER

Explore the amazing underground formations of caves – and get ready to experience a different world.

How to earn your badge
1. Take part in at least four trips to at least two different cave systems. You must make each visit as a member of a properly led group.
2. Keep a record of your trips and the routes you followed.
3. Develop a good knowledge of the caving and cave conservation codes. Show your assessor that you're aware of the environmental issues around caving.

❶ Your leader will need to check the activity rules in chapter nine of Policy, Organisation and Rules and the Adventurous Activity Permit Scheme.

CHEF

When your fellow Scouts come back from a long day of activities and challenges, they'll need a meal that can sustain them. This badge gives you the opportunity to plan and execute a menu that everyone can enjoy.

How to earn your badge

1. Plan a menu for a weekend event for between four and six people. Include the quantities you'll need and any dietary needs of the group for cultural, religious or medical reasons.
2. Show how and where to shop for the food and the best way to transport it.
3. Show how to store food properly, hygienically and in ways that prevent food poisoning. Explain what you might need to consider if you're using an indoor kitchen or a camp kitchen.
4. Cook and serve at least one of the meals from your menu. The meal must be at least two courses and can be prepared on an open fire on camp or in a kitchen.
5. Demonstrate the best way to clear up afterwards. Clearing up should include washing up utensils, pots and pans, disposing of rubbish and leftover food in a way that prevents vermin or disease.

Top tips
You can complete the steps using an indoor kitchen or outdoors cooking. You can use a gas or wood fire outdoors.

You can gain the Chef badge twice, once by completing the steps using an indoor kitchen and once for outdoors.

CIRCUS SKILLS

Be the star attraction at the big top as you surprise and entertain everyone with your awesome circus skills.

How to earn your badge
Before you attempt this badge, have a look through the skills. You should make sure you're fit and able to both enjoy and master the skills you choose. For example, you may want to make sure you practice balancing for wire walking.
1. Select two skills from the table below. The two skills must be from different lists.

Aerial	Balance	Manipulative
trapeze	trick-cycling	cigar boxes
roman rings	stilts	club swinging
aerial ladder	ladder	devilsticks
aerial rope	tightrope	diablo.
wire walking.	wire walking	
	perch	
	roller bolo	
	slack-rope.	

Ground	Clowning	Juggling	Spinning
handstands	make up	with three	yo-yo
tumbling	costume	objects or more.	poi spinning
acrobatics			rhythmic
			gymnastics
			(twirling
			ribbon)
			spinning
			plates.

2. Carry on putting effort into your two selected skills and show some achievement. Someone with experience should guide you throughout.
3. Demonstrate your two selected skills in front of an audience.
4. Find out things about circus life and talk about these with an adult.
5. Watch at least two circus or street performance events. Talk about what you saw.

Your leader will give you instructions on using the equipment safely. You must listen carefully and follow these instructions. Your leader must also follow procedures in line with The Scout Association's health and safety policy.

Top tips
Joining a circus skills workshop, or another course outside of Scouts, is a great way to learn your chosen skills.

CLIMBER

Climbing like a pro isn't just about physical ability – it's about communicating with your team and using the right equipment for the job. Not only that, it's an awesome feeling to get to the top!

How to earn your badge

1. Show that you know the rope types used for rock climbing. Explain how to coil and maintain them.
2. Show that you know how to fit a climbing helmet and harness and how to tie in correctly.
3. Show you understand the calls used in climbing.
4. Show that you know how to abseil down a face. It should usually be at least 10 metres high. Alternatively, you can take part in a climbing-like activity, such as crate stacking or high ropes, and show you know about the safety equipment used.
5. Take part in four or more separate climbs. Your climbs should either be on artificial walls of grade 4+/5 or natural faces up to 'difficult' standard. You could do a mixture of both, using a different route for each climb. Either way, an experienced climber must supervise your climbs and evaluate your ability.

6. Explain the safety rules for climbing on both natural and artificial rock faces.
7. Show that you're aware of environmental issues around climbing on natural rock faces.
8. Explain how to care for the equipment you used. Also, explain what you should look out for when equipment is nearing the end of its life.

Top tips
Remember, you're not expected to lead the rock climbs. You only need to be a competent second or use a top rope.

Your Leader will need to make sure the activity rules in chapter nine of Policy, Organisation and Rules and the Adventurous Activity Permit Scheme are being followed.

COMMUNICATOR

Communication can help us
reach out to more people, from
longer distances and using a
wide range of languages. Work
towards your Communicator badge and help bring
people closer together.

How to earn your badge
Choose from one of the five options. Then
complete all the tasks under your chosen option.

Option 1: radio communication
You automatically gain this activity badge if you
already hold, or reach the standard of these
qualifications:
- Radio Amateur Licence (Foundation,
  Intermediate or Full)
- Marine Radio Operator's Certificate of
  Competence and Authority to Operate
- Flight Radio Telephone Operator's Licence.

If not, complete all of these.
1. Log 25 different amateur radio stations.
   Note the date, time, call sign, frequency,
   readability and location. You may include some
   broadcast stations.
2. Show how to tune a simple
   communications receiver.

3. Give an example of a typical greetings message.
4. Explain in simple terms how radio waves travel around the world. Learn the more commonly used HF and VHF amateur frequency bands.
5. Learn the phonetic alphabet and define at least eight international Q code signals.
6. Show that you can recognise call signs from the UK and near continent.
7. Visit an amateur radio station.
8. Learn the regulations governing the use of amateur radio equipment.

Option 2: communication codes
1. Send and receive a short message by Morse code or semaphore at a rate of five words per minute.
2. Show that you know the proper procedure for sending and receiving a message.
3. Learn the international phonetic alphabet and define at least eight international Q code signals.
4. Construct a simple Morse code oscillator and send a short message.

Option 3: mobile and internet communication
1. Show you know how to use your mobile safely and how to keep it safe.
2. Learn the meaning of these terms: SMS, MMS, 3G, 4G, WAP and Bluetooth.

3. Send a creative text, multimedia or video message to invite a friend to a Scouts event.
4. Manage a mobile phone address book and set up groups of contacts.
5. Show you can text accurately at a rate of 50 characters per minute.
6. Show you know the meaning of some popular chat abbreviations.
7. Share photos and videos of a Scouting activity you've been involved with, using available technology.
8. Manage an email address book and set up groups of contacts.

Option 4: foreign languages

Complete these tasks in any foreign language:
1. Carry on a simple conversation for about 10 minutes.
2. Write a letter of around 150 words.
3. After a few minutes of study, translate a paragraph of basic text.
4. Act as an interpreter for a visitor who does not speak your native language.
5. Communicate with a person who does not speak your native language.

Option 5: translator

Complete these tasks in a recognised sign language, such as Makaton or BSL:

1. Carry out a simple conversation for about 10 minutes.
2. Use sign language to describe a Scouting experience to another person.
3. Act as a translator for a short conversation between a sign language user and someone with no sign language experience.
4. Invite a sign language user to talk to your Troop about what it's like to have impaired hearing or speech. Help by translating for them during their visit.

CRAFT

With practice and patience, you can develop the skills to make really amazing items that people will love.

How to earn your badge
To achieve this badge you need to make or decorate one or more articles using, whenever possible, original design ideas.

You should discuss this project beforehand with a member of your leadership team. It should take around six hours to complete the project.

Here are some items you could make:
- A container using basket making, woodturning, pottery, embroidery on plastic canvas, glass blowing or fibreglass construction.
- A belt, bag, wall hanging, tablemat or waistcoat by weaving, macramé, beadwork or from leather.
- An item of clothing or soft furnishing, by sewing or knitting. You may follow a pattern.

- You could decorate clothing or soft furnishing (such as a cushion or tablecloth) using embroidery, tapestry, lace making, tie and dye, wax and dye or fabric paints.
- A picture, using techniques like mosaic, staining glass, quilting, calligraphy, pyrography, pressed flowers, fabric collage, printing with potato, lino, string, drypoint, aquatint or silkscreen.
- Decorate a material (such as wood, metal or glass) by engraving or etching. You could even try painting metal with cold enamel.
- Make a decorative item through candle making, arranging flowers, carving (using materials such as wood, slate, stone or soap), fly tying, jewellery making, pewterwork, copper or silversmithing, stone polishing, stone masonry or sculpture.
- Make a small item of furniture.
- Decorate a cake for a special occasion.

Alternatively, you can do any other project of a similar skill level. Just agree it beforehand with your leadership team.

! You must take care with all tools and materials to avoid injury.

CYCLIST

Have you ever heard the phrase 'you never forget how to ride a bicycle'? It's true – but the journeys you go on while you're cycling are just as memorable. Make sure your skills are up to scratch so you need never miss out on a cycling adventure.

How to earn your badge
There are two parts to achieving this badge. Complete all tasks for part one.
1. Use a bicycle that is properly equipped. Keep it in good working order for at least six months.
2. Show that you can carry out essential maintenance and repairs, including:
   - checking and adjusting the brakes
   - checking and adjusting the gear change
   - adjusting the seat and handlebars to a correct height
   - removing a wheel and locating and repairing at puncture
   - checking and adjusting your cycle helmet
   - maintaining a set of lights.

For part two of this activity badge, choose one of these options then complete all the tasks for that option.

Option 1: road cycling

You can automatically complete option 1 if you gain Bikeability Level 2 or 3. Otherwise, here's what you need to do for this option.

1. Explain what extra precautions you should take when cycling in the dark or in wet weather. Show you understand why motor vehicles take longer to stop in the wet.
2. Learn the basics of first aid and what to do if an accident happens.
3. Develop a working knowledge of map reading. Orientate a map using a compass or conspicuous features. Estimate distances and times taken to travel.
4. Plan and carry out an all-day cycle ride of at least 40 kilometres (25 miles).
5. Complete one of these:
   - Show you can control a cycle along a slalom course.
   - Show you understand the Highway Code, including road signs and helmet use.

Option 2: off-road cycling

1. Show you understand the Mountain Bike Code of Conduct.
2. Show you can control your cycle over different types of terrain.

3. Show you're aware of the damage that may be caused to the environment through careless cycling across the countryside.
4. Learn the basics of first aid, including the treatment of hypothermia and find out what to do in the case of an accident.
5. Gain a working knowledge of map reading. Orientate a map using a compass or conspicuous features. Estimate distances and times taken to travel.
6. Plan and carry out an all-day ride of at least 30 kilometres (20 miles).

Option 3: external qualifications
You can complete option 3 if you reach one of these standards:
- The Gold Trix Award of the British Schools Cycling Association
- Level 3 Go-MTB Award from Cycling Scotland, Sustrans, CTC or Scottish Cycling MBLA

You must always wear a cycle helmet when riding your bike. The only exception is if you're Sikh and you wear a turban.

Top tips
You might find these websites useful:
dft.gov.uk/bikeability
bsca.org.uk
cyclingscotland.org

sustrans.org.uk
ctc.org.uk
britishcycling.org.uk/scotland
mbla.org.uk

DIY

Would you like to be handy
around the house? Learn how to
deal with emergencies and
tackle DIY projects – you'll be in
the good books with your family and achieve
something to be proud of.

How to earn your badge
1. Show you can work safely and know about
   the following:
   - hazard symbols and signs (for dangers such
     as toxic, flammable, irritant, electrical danger
     or slippery surface)
   - safety equipment (such as goggles, gloves,
     masks, ear defenders)
   - how and where to turn off mains
     supplies (such as water, electricity and gas)
     to the house.
2. Learn how to safely isolate individual electrical
   circuits at the consumer unit. This includes
   letting other users know that work is being
   carried out.

3. Show or explain how you would deal with four DIY emergencies for example:
- unblocking a sink
- patching a leaking pipe
- adjusting the float arm of a cistern
- hinge a door back in place
- fixing a door bell ringer
- stabilising a wobbly stair rail
- repairing a tear in clothes or upholstery
- removing common stains eg ink, wine and coffee.

4. Take an active part in two major DIY projects, indoors or outside. You could:
- prepare and paint, paper or tile the walls of a room
- prepare and paint woodwork or furniture
- fit a curtain track and hang curtains
- make a freestanding storage unit or put up shelves
- cover a floor with vinyl overlay, lino, tiles or carpet
- hang a door and fit or repair locks and other door furniture
- lay a patio, decking or path
- build a low wall, barbecue, gate or fence
- carry out routine service checks on a car, then clean and polish the car.

Alternatively, you could do any other projects of a similar skill level. Agree what you'll do with an adult who is skilled in the relevant areas.

DRAGON BOATING

Dragon Boating is an exciting water sport. It's a Chinese tradition that goes back over 2,000 years and involves a crew of up to 20! Pull together and work as a team to achieve this badge.

How to earn your badge
1. Learn the safety rules, capsize drill and the water buddy system.
2. Learn the procedures for loading, numbering off, stopping, bracing the boat, forward and backward paddling.
3. Learn the instructions and commands issued by The Dragon Boat Racing Association.
4. Carry out practice training sessions for a minimum of two hours. Practice a race over a distance of at least 250 metres.
5. Take part in a competitive or timed dragon boat event over a course of at least 250 metres.

Top tips
You can use a bell boat.

You must check and comply with the activity rules in chapter nine of Policy, Organisation and Rules and the Adventurous Activity Permit Scheme.

ELECTRONICS

Are you a bright spark? Work towards your Electronics activity badge and create clever systems and circuits that support our modern lives.

How to earn your badge

1. Identify a number of common electronic components that are shown to you. Explain, in simple terms, the functions they perform in electronic circuits.
2. Describe the systems used for marking components with their values. Demonstrate by identifying the values of resistors and capacitors by their markings. Explain the importance of the rating of a component.
3. Show that you know the symbols used to represent common components in circuit diagrams. Show how to identify the polarity of a diode and a specific pin number on an integrated circuit.
4. Show that you're aware of the safe working practices to be followed when handling electronic components, circuit boards and when soldering.
5. Use a multimeter to measure voltage, current and resistance in a simple circuit. Explain the relationship between these values.

6. Talk about the main differences in the operation of digital and analogue circuits.

7. Construct three simple circuits. One of these should be based mainly on digital electronics. They can be from a book or magazine, or you can design the circuits yourself. If possible, at least one of the circuits should be soldered using either stripboard or a custom-made printed circuit board.

8. Explain the principles behind the operation of each circuit and the typical values of voltage and current found in each.

9. Explain the possible uses of the three circuits you built.

10. Talk about the uses and benefits of electronics in everyday life. Explain how electronics can be used to improve lives.

ENTERTAINER

Get ready to accept a standing ovation – showcase your talent and have fun creating a great piece of entertainment.

How to earn your badge
Choose one of the options. Then, as part of a group, complete all tasks to achieve this badge.

Option 1
1. Write and plan some original entertainment. It could involve a campfire or stage routine involving mime, drama, music, storytelling or conjuring. Alternatively, it could take the form of a presentation featuring sketches, film, slides, tapes, photography or sound recordings.
2. Rehearse the entertainment and make sure everyone has a job to do. You might need actors, a producer, a stage manager, front of house or a publicity manager.
3. Present the entertainment to an audience at a school, for your Troop or at a parents' evening.

Option 2
Take an active part in a Scout show or another production. You'll need to commit to regular rehearsals.

ENVIRONMENTAL CONSERVATION

We only have one world, and you can help look after it.
By completing your Environmental Conservation activity badge, you can protect our environment and our future.

How to earn your badge
1. Find out about an environmental issue that is important to your local community. It might be linked to:
   - recycling and conservation
   - energy efficiency in the home or your meeting place
   - the building of new homes and local land use
   - water, light, thermal, air or beach pollution
   - coastal erosion
   - the impact of tourism on the local environment.
2. Take part in an activity or project that improves local conservation. It could take place during a weekend conservation camp or you could spread it over at least five weekly sessions. You could look at:
   - recycling
   - reducing energy usage or renewable energy
   - protecting important habitats or wildlife

- pollution
- erosion
- flooding.

3. Get involved in a campaign to make others aware of an environmental issue. You could write to your MP and other local agencies or speak to a community group.

Top tips
Why not offer a recycling service for things like printer cartridges, tools or glasses?

EQUESTRIAN

Perfect your walk, trot and canter. Showcase your horse riding skills for the Equestrian badge.

Here's what you need to do to earn this badge.

1. Riding
   - Show you can catch a pony from a field or stable and tack up for riding.
   - Walk, trot and canter a pony.
   - Jump over small fences.
2. Grooming and care
   - Groom your pony correctly and explain why it is necessary.
   - Show you know how to take care of saddlery and other equipment.
3. Horse health
   - Find out about some of the basic health issues affecting horses and ponies, including worms and laminitis.
   - Show you have a basic knowledge of grass management. Show you recognise poisonous plants and the results of overgrazing.
4. Safety
   - Talk about road safety for riding.
   - Explain why you need a hat, body protector, stirrup and other safety equipment.

FARMING

When you know how to work
the land and grow your own,
you can learn to be really
self-reliant. Grab your wellies
and start producing your own food and other
supplies.

How to earn your badge
Choose one of the three options below.
Complete the tasks for your chosen option
to achieve this badge.

Option 1
1. Learn about farming practices in your area.
2. Find out about the organisation, as well as
   the daily and seasonal operations, of a farm
   of your choice. Make a note of practices relating
   to livestock, crops, cultivation, rotation,
   machinery and labour force.
3. Find photos to demonstrate the changes in
   farming practices that have taken place over a
   number of years. Explain the reasons for these.

Option 2

1. Cultivate an area of garden or an allotment for a specific length of time. Agree this beforehand with your leadership team.
2. Show you're successful in growing:
   - three kinds of hardy annual flower
   - three kinds of vegetable
   - two kinds of bulbs, herbaceous plants, flowering shrubs or roses.
3. Keep a record of the work you've done and the results you achieved. This could include height records of the flowers, for example.

Option 3

Keep any kind of livestock for at least three months.

- look after farm animals or birds, and learn how they should be housed, fed and bred as well as their economic uses. Show how to handle them safely and learn about animal welfare.
- manage a hive. Bring in some of the honey you produce.

An experienced adult will need to oversee the activities.

FIRE SAFETY

When fire starts, knowing how to act – and doing it quickly – can save lives. Learn the essentials of fire safety by working towards this badge.

How to earn your badge

1. Explain what action should be taken and why, if you discover a fire has broken out in the home or at camp.
2. Explain the process of combustion. Find out about the effects of smoke and heat and how to act in smoke.
3. Be aware of dangers in the home and the fire precautions necessary for:
   - oil heaters and open solid fuel fires
   - portable electric fires
   - drying clothes
   - electric wiring and fuses
   - smoking paraphernalia, particularly matches
   - uses of household gas, including gas fires
   - party decorations and candles
   - closing doors and windows
   - using BBQs.
4. Explain the benefits of installing smoke detectors. Describe the best places to install them.

5. Learn what the dangers of campfires are and what precautions should be taken.
6. Find out about the causes of heath and grass fires.
7. Learn how to make an emergency call for the fire service.
8. Identify different fire extinguisher types such as water, dry powder, foam and carbon dioxide. Explain what kinds of fire they should be used on.
9. Find out what to do if a person's clothes are on fire.
10. Talk to your family about what to do in the event of a fire at home.

Top tips
You could take part in a course with your local fire and rescue service to complete this badge.

FORESTER

Find out about how to manage and identify trees, and help preserve our woodland areas.

How to earn your badge

1. Identify at least eight common types of tree that grow in your area, including both deciduous and coniferous.
2. Find out how to identify trees using identification keys.
3. Prepare the soil and successfully transplant a young tree.
4. Find out how both natural woodland and commercial forests are managed. Be aware of the damage these areas may be exposed to from wind, frost, fire and animals.
5. Show how to select, use and care for forestry equipment, and know the safety issues involved.
6. Show how to fell and trim out a tree or lay a hedge.

! You must be trained by a skilled person and understand the correct use of axes and saws. You must also be supervised by an adult at all times.

FUNDRAISING

Charities rely on donations to keep going. By taking on the Fundraising activity badge, you can help them do more work.

You'll also inspire people to start supporting good causes, including The Scout Association.

How to earn your badge

1. Identify and organise a fundraising initiative for either:
   - The Scout Association, to promote and grow Scouting nationally, or your local group to pay for something like new equipment or a new roof. You could even fundraise for both.
   - another UK registered charity.
2. Think of a short reason that tells potential donors about your chosen cause. It must be inspiring and clear to raise the most money.
3. Set a target and a date by which you'll have raised the money. We suggest a minimum of £100.
4. Write a short report about your fundraising challenge and submit it to your leader, Troop Forum or Patrol Leaders' Council. Detail the cost versus the amount raised and give three top tips that could help other fundraisers.

Top tips

You might like to take part in a fundraising event to reach your target, like:

- a challenge you have set and organised yourself, making sure you comply with all regulations
- something you organise, such as a fete, restaurant evening or car wash.

Always remember to collect Gift Aid, if possible. Think about other ways to you can raise the most money.

Make sure you follow the appropriate rules and make use of different tools available for fundraising.

GEOCACHING

Would you like to be a treasure hunter? Use GPS technology to uncover secret caches in mystery locations.

Here's what you need to do earn this badge.

1. Show that you know about the Global Positioning System (GPS) by explaining:
   - how it works
   - ownership and control of the system
   - its benefits to society
   - what factors affect its accuracy.
2. Programme a handheld GPS receiver to:
   - find your location (grid reference, plus latitude and longitude) and record it
   - enter the grid reference of a local landmark and navigate to the waypoint
   - enter the latitude and longitude coordinates of a nearby point and navigate to the waypoint. Be sure to check the accuracy.
   - walk on a bearing using the GPS and a map.
3. Show that you know the difference between Ordnance Survey, and latitude and longitude coordinates.
4. Using an Ordnance Survey map (1:25000 or 1:50000 scale) to plan a route of at least 4km that contains a minimum of 10 waypoints. Talk about the features and challenges along the

route. Programme the route into a handheld GPS and take the journey.

5. Sign up to a geocaching website. Find out about geocaching and show that you understand what's involved in both locating and placing a geocache.

6. Show that you understand the safety and environmental aspects of geocaching, such as the Highway Code, Countryside Code and the Geocaching Association of Great Britain (GAGB) guidelines.

7. Find five geocaches using a GPS. At least three geocaches must be 'multi-caches', with at least two waypoints. Talk about the GPS receiver's accuracy of information provided.

8. With the help of an adult:
   - plan, assemble and hide two caches, one of which should be a multi-cache. Make sure the location is suitable and that other navigators have proper access to the land and terrain.
   - either submit your caches to a geocaching website or give the details to other Scouts so they can find the caches.

Your leader will need to make sure you follow the activity rules in chapter nine of Policy, Organisation and Rules and the Adventurous Activity Permit Scheme. If you are aged 13 or under, an adult will also need to sign up to the geocaching website on behalf of your Troop.

GLOBAL ISSUES

This badge links to the Global Goals that people and governments all over the world are trying to achieve to make the world a better place. By doing this badge and learning about important global issues, you can explore the world around you and understand the role you can play in making it a better place.

How to earn your badge

1. Identify where your clothing or other belongings have been made. With other Scouts, talk about why companies might choose to have the items made in other countries. What are the advantages and disadvantages of overseas production?
2. Investigate a recent natural disaster by looking at photos, news articles or videos online. Decide in small groups what five things were needed to help people after the disaster. Decide as a Troop how best you can help when a natural disaster happens.
3. Find out about an international sporting event and discuss with your Troop how sporting events can contribute to international peace and understanding.

4. In small groups, learn about an international health issue and use a creative way to share what you have learnt with your Troop. Issues could include Malaria, Ebola, HIV and Aids.

5. Think about the rights that we have in the UK (like the right to vote, the right to go to school and equal gender rights). Compare these with the rights a Scout in another country might have.

Top tips

Bookbridge is a charity set up by European Scouts to support young people in many different countries access education through learning centres. They have developed resources that may help you to complete this badge.

HILL WALKER

Increase your stamina, improve
your planning and preparation
skills, and explore the vast open
countryside. The Hill Walker
badge for Scouts helps you prepare for an epic,
uphill journey.

How to earn your badge

1. With others, plan at least five one-day journeys
   of at least 14km in hilly country. At least three of
   these should be in areas defined as terrain one
   and be led by a permit holder.
2. Using Ordnance Survey maps, complete all the
   information you need to plan the route for each
   journey.
3. Learn how to summon help in an emergency.
   Make sure you know what In Touch system will
   be used.
4. Make sure you know the different types of
   hazards you might come across. There might be
   water hazards, unstable ground, changeable
   weather conditions or other dangers.
5. Before setting out, list the equipment that should
   be taken and explain how to use them correctly.
   This includes:
   - spare food and safety or emergency equipment
   - what you should wear
   - what you should carry.

6. Complete your planned journeys. Take turns in leading the group for part of each journey. Keep a log of your journeys.

7. During the journey, show how you use the map and compass.

8. Show you're aware of ways to preserve the natural environment, such as avoiding erosion and conserving wildlife habitats.

9. Show that you're aware of developments in technology, such as the Global Positioning System (GPS), digital mapping or waterproof maps.

10. Show that you know the publication Safety on Mountains, published by the British Mountaineering Council.

This badge should be worked towards in terrain one and below and in summer conditions.

Top tip
You can find useful information about route cards on our website. Visit **scouts.org.uk/ supportresources**

HOBBIES

If you regularly take part in a hobby and there's no specific badge for it, this is the badge you need.

How to earn your badge
Choose one of the two options below. Complete the tasks for your chosen option to achieve this badge.

Option 1
1. Take up a hobby or interest that you do not already have an activity badge for.
2. Keep a record of your hobby for at least four months.

Option 2
1. Make a collection or study of objects for at least four months. You could collect books or magazines, films, cards, key rings, figurines or similar.
2. Talk to your Patrol Leader or your Troop about the collection or study you chose. Explain why you chose your objects and what you like about them.

Top tips
You can earn more than one Hobbies Badge. A hobby is an activity done regularly in leisure time for enjoyment. This could include reading.

INTERNATIONAL

Broaden your horizons and
explore the culture and traditions
of another country. The International
badge will take you on a journey and
help you learn from different communities.

How to earn your badge
1. Find out about the World Scout Movement's
   history and what it does today. Complete a quiz
   in teams to see who in your Troop knows the
   most about the World Scout Movement and
   discuss what you think World Scouting could do
   in the future.
2. Take part in a traditional craft or creative activity
   from another country.
3. In a language other than your own,
   introduce yourself and say a few basic,
   useful, everyday phrases.
4. Take part in one of these events individually or
   with the Troop and report back to other Scouts:
   • Jamboree On The Internet (JOTI) or Jamboree
     On The Air (JOTA)
   • an international camp held in the UK or abroad
   • a link to Scouts in another country.

Top tips
For number 2, traditional crafts from other countries
might include hieroglyphics, Chinese calligraphy,

traditional tribal dress or masks, musical instruments, leatherwork, jewellery and accessories or woodcraft.

LIBRARIAN

Did you know the British Library holds over 57 million records of books, manuscripts and other publications? Think you could sort and search them all? First thing's first – gain your Librarian activity badge and put a world of knowledge at your fingertips.

How to earn your badge
1. Show that you know how to look after books and e-readers.
2. Show that you can use a library catalogue.
3. Explain how fiction and non-fiction books are arranged on the shelves. Why are they treated differently?
4. Learn what is meant by a reference book or material. Use some of these references to gather information for a journey with a purpose:
   - leisure leaflet or webpage
   - bus or train timetable
   - almanac or a who's who
   - gazetteer or Yellow Pages
5. Show how you would search for information using the internet.

6. Talk to your assessor about:
   - books you have read and why you enjoyed them
   - information you found from books or websites
   - getting books on the internet for e-readers.

LIFESAVER

Would you know what to do if someone's life was in danger? This badge can help you to learn the invaluable skills and techniques used in an emergency.

How to earn your badge

1. Explain and, if you can, show how you would carry out a rescue from water using these methods:
   - shout
   - reach
   - throwing a buoyant aid
   - throwing a rope
   - wade.
2. Reach the standard of one of these:
   - Royal Lifesaving Society UK (RLSS UK) Rookie Lifeguard Gold Level 1 award
   - Royal Lifesaving Society UK (RLSS UK) Survive and Save Silver Medallion award.

3. Explain and, if you can, show what you would do if:
- a person fell through ice
- a pet fell through ice.

LOCAL KNOWLEDGE

If you know your local area like the back of your hand, or you'd like to explore all its routes, roads and useful places, this badge is for you.

How to earn your badge
Choose one of these three options, depending on where you live. Then complete all the tasks.

Option 1: rural and suburban areas
1. Show that you know the local area surrounding your home or Scout Headquarters, up to a radius of 2 kilometres in suburban districts and 5 kilometres in rural districts. Locate as many as you can of these:
- doctors, veterinary surgeons, dentists, hospitals and ambulance station
- fire station, police station, garages, shopping centres, retail parks and convenience stores
- main bus stops, railway stations and local routes of buses and trains

- local Scout Headquarters, public parks, theatres, sports and leisure complexes and cinemas
- places of worship, museums, schools, colleges and local government buildings
- local routes that take you to the nearest motorway or national routes.

2. Use a street map to point out six locations from step 1. From your home or Scout Headquarters, show the quickest route to one of the places.

Option 2: urban areas

1. Gain a general knowledge of what parts of the country are served from your local airport, mainline railway and coach stations.
2. Find out how to reach the local airport, mainline railway and coach stations, and major tourist attractions from your Scout Headquarters or home.
3. Show how to use a map of your district. Use it to point out any six places of interest. Show how to get to these places from your Scout Headquarters or home.
4. Give clear directions to a place of interest 8 kilometres away, to a person travelling by car or public transport.
5. Find out which major local roads link to the motorway and A-road network and the main cities these roads serve.

Option 3: heritage

1. Study an aspect of national history, local history or family heritage. Exhibit or present the results to other people.
2. Over a period agreed with your leader, get involved in a project to help preserve some aspect of national or local heritage.

MARTIAL ARTS

Martial arts can help you become disciplined, confident and calm under pressure. Work towards this badge to show how you've improved in one of many martial arts areas.

How to earn your badge

1. Take part in a regular martial arts activity that's recognised by your sports council for at least six months. Show how you've improved by at least one level over that period.
2. Take part in a competition or demonstration and talk about your performance with an instructor.

Top tip

You can earn this badge by taking part in aikido, judo, ju-jitsu, karate, kendo, sombo, taekwondo, tang soo do or wrestling.

Here are the national sports councils, where you can find more recognised martial arts:

Sport England **sportengland.org**
Sport Scotland **sportscotland.org.uk**
Sport Wales **sportwales.org.uk**
Sport Northern Ireland **sportni.net**

MASTER AT ARMS

If you'd like to shoot an arrow with precision, a rifle with accuracy or fence with finesse, why not try going for your Master at Arms activity badge?

How to earn your badge

If you have completed the NSRA Youth Proficiency Scheme in Air Rifle or Air Pistol shooting you automatically earn this badge.

Otherwise, here's what you need to do.

1. Attend regular training sessions in a relevant activity like fencing, shooting or archery. Show how you've improved in technique. You should train for at least six sessions.
2. Learn the safety rules associated with your activity and show how to follow them.
3. Take part in your chosen activity at an officially supervised contest. Afterwards, talk to the instructor about your performance and how you can improve.

> ❗ Your leader must make sure you're following
> the activity rules in Policy, Organisation and
> Rules relating to shooting and archery.

MECHANIC

Get your motor running with a
few skills of the trade. The
Mechanic activity badge helps
you learn to fix engines in one of
four specialist areas.

How to earn your badge
Choose one of the four options. Then complete all
tasks for your chosen option.

Option 1: motor car
1. Learn the principles of operating an internal
   combustion engine. Make sure you understand
   the function of the clutch, gearbox and rear
   axle differential.
2. Show how to check and refill the windscreen
   wash bottle of a car.
3. Show how to change a bulb at the front and in
   the rear light cluster of a car.
4. Show how to check the level of water in the
   radiator, 'top up' the radiator and explain the
   importance of anti-freeze.
5. Show how to check tyre pressures and inflate a
   tyre correctly.

6. Remove and replace a road wheel.
7. Explain what to look for when checking that a tyre conforms to the legal requirement.
   Find out why cross and radial ply tyres should not be mixed on the same axle.
8. Show how to change a wiper blade.
9. Explain the outline requirements for an MOT road test.

Option 2: power boat

1. Complete one of these activities:
   - Discuss the principles and performance of several types of motorboat engines, other than two-stroke. Show that you know the maintenance needed for a familiar type of marine internal combustion engine, other than two-stroke.
   - Assist with the maintenance, dismantle, service and reassemble an outboard engine. Show how to fit it properly to the transom of a boat. Explain how to detect minor faults in starting and running whilst afloat.
2. Complete one of these activities:
   - As driver or mechanic member of a power boat's crew, help to prepare the boat for a voyage by checking the engine for possible minor faults, checking the fuel supply and pump and mustering the fire-fighting equipment. Show you know how to leave the engine in a proper manner and how to drain

the engine in an emergency.

- Check the engine of a motorboat in preparation for a cruise or expedition, making sure there is fuel that is stored safely, an adequate tool kit and effective fire-fighting apparatus. Accompany the expedition, either as the mechanic or assistant, and be fully or jointly responsible for the operation, care and maintenance of the engine throughout.

Option 3: aircraft

1. Learn the basic principles of one these component parts and be able to point them out:
   - an aircraft piston engine
   - an aircraft gas turbine engine.
2. Learn the basic principles of flight and airframe construction of a fixed wing aircraft.
3. Learn and then demonstrate Aircraft Marshalling signals used by day and night.
4. Show you can carry out any four of these:
   - replenishing a light aircraft fuel and oil system safely
   - rigging and de-rigging a glider
   - picketing a light aircraft
   - changing plugs on a light aircraft engine
   - inspecting aircraft main and tail or nose wheel tyres for serviceability
   - repairing a small tear in the fabric surface of a light aircraft or glider

- checking the control system of a light aircraft or glider for correct sense of movement.

Option 4: motorcycle or scooter
1. Learn the principles of operating a two-stroke or four-stroke internal combustion engine. Learn about the function of the clutch, gearbox, carburettor and transmission of a motorcycle.
2. Remove, clean and check the gap of a sparking plug.
3. Check and top up the level of the engine oil.
4. Explain how to adjust the tension of the final drive chain.
5. Show how you change a bulb at the front and in the rear light cluster.
6. Show how you would check tyre pressures and inflate a tyre correctly.
7. Remove and replace a road wheel.
8. Explain what to look for when checking that a tyre conforms to the legal requirement.
9. Explain the outline requirements for an MOT road test.

Top tips
Remember to follow the manufacturer's guidelines at all times.

MEDIA RELATIONS AND MARKETING

Help raise the profile of The Scout Association and pick up some fantastic skills. Media relations and marketing is a really important part of any organisation and it's interesting too.

How to earn your badge
Choose from three of these activities to achieve this badge.

1. Produce and give a presentation about Scouting. Use audio and visual media and think about how you can make it relevant to people not involved in Scouting.

2. Write a press release about a Scout event that has taken place. Send it to your local Media Development Manager so that they can get it published in the local press, radio station or community website.

3. Find out about local media outlets such as radio, TV, newspapers and online. Find out what their target audience is and work out a storyline that they might be interested in featuring.

4. Prepare and present an audio or video package about a Scouting event or activity. The report should be accurate, informative and reflect the adventure of Scouting.
5. Prepare a creative display about your Troop or Group that can be exhibited in your local library, information centre or public place.
6. Interview a local public figure or someone in the local news, such as a church leader, politician or celebrity and present the interview to your Troop. Get some advice from your Leader before contacting the person.
7. Produce some media which can be used within Scouting, such as a district newsletter story or a piece of website content.

METEOROLOGIST

Rain or shine, wind or snow –
show everyone what you know
about weather.

How to earn your badge

1. Explain how each of these are measured:
   - wind force and direction
   - cloud type and extent
   - temperature
   - pressure
   - rainfall
   - humidity.
2. Record the weather conditions every day
   for two weeks or once a week for three
   months. Use equipment like a rain gauge
   or an outdoor thermometer.
3. Identify different cloud types. Describe how
   they are formed.
4. What do 'warm' and 'cold' air masses in
   summer and winter do to the typical weather in
   your area? Describe the effects of land and sea.
5. Explain how weather forecasts are created.
6. Show that you understand a synoptic weather
   map, including fronts and isobars. Explain how
   the measurements in step 1 relate to the map.

MODEL MAKER

Build miniature structures with amazing precision by working towards your Model Maker badge. This is how big companies prototype everything from cars to buildings, so give it a go and learn a useful skill in design.

How to earn your badge

Choose one of these five options. Then complete all steps for your chosen option.

Option 1

1. Choose one of these activities:
   - Build a model using a plastic or white metal kit or pre-cast figures.
   - Design and construct a model from a wood, plastic or metal construction set, such as Lego or Meccano.
2. Show that you know the different types of kits or parts available in the material you chose.
3. Talk about the experience of building the model with a knowledgeable adult.

Option 2
1. Build a model aeroplane, using a kit if you want to. It must meet one of these target flight performances:
   - A hand-launched glider must fly for 25 seconds.
   - A tow-launched glider must fly for 45 seconds, with 50 metres maximum line length.
   - A rubber-powered aircraft must fly for 30 seconds.
   - An engine-powered aircraft must fly for 45 seconds, with 15 seconds maximum motor run.
   - A control line aircraft must show a smooth take off and landing, with three laps of level flight at about 2 metres, with a climb and dive.
2. Talk about the experience of building and flying the model with a knowledgeable adult.

Option 3
1. Build an electric or engine-powered model boat or yacht at least 45 cm in length. Show that it's capable of maintaining a straight course of at least 25 metres. You can use a kit if you like.
2. Talk about the experience of building the model with a knowledgeable adult.

Option 4

1. Choose one of these two activities:
   - Build an electric slot car racer. Drive it a minimum distance of 122 metres on any track, without stopping or leaving the slot more than four times.
   - Build a free running car of any type. Show that it can run for at least 18 metres. Airscrew drive is allowed and you can use a kit if you like.
2. Talk about the experience of building the model with a knowledgeable adult.

Option 5

1. Build a model coach or wagon. Show that it can run properly behind a scale locomotive.
2. Build a scaled scenic model, such as a station or farmhouse for a railway layout. You can use a kit if you like.
3. Talk about the experience of building your models with a knowledgeable adult.

MY FAITH

If you have a faith, enjoy developing a deeper understanding of your beliefs and how they guide you through your life.

How to earn your badge
If you have been confirmed, had your bat mitzvah or bar mitzvah or a similar faith life experience, you only need to take part in a Scouting activity relating to your faith to qualify for your badge.

Otherwise, here's what you need to do.
1. Take an active part in your place of worship. You could get involved in community work, take a special part in services or celebrations or follow a training or study programme.
2. Find out more about the origins of your faith. Share what you find out with others in the Troop.
3. Explore something about the history of your faith at a local, national or international level. You could learn about influential people, or visit a shrine or other holy place.
4. Explain to an adult some of the teachings of your faith. Explain how these affect the way you live your life.

NATURALIST

We rely on the natural world for our very survival. This badge will demonstrate your impact and role in preserving it.

How to earn your badge

1. With appropriate permission, spend at least one day at one of these locations and investigate the wildlife and plants found there:
   - woodland or parkland
   - down land
   - moor land
   - seashore or sand dune
   - hedgerow
   - roadside verge
   - stream, river or canal
   - small pond
   - wetland or marshland.
2. Tell a knowledgeable adult what you discovered. Show them your field notes, sketches, photographs or maps.
3. Find out more about a plant, animal or particular wildlife from your chosen location.
4. Discuss what you found out, giving sources for information from places like museums, field guides or the internet.
5. Discuss how human activities or land management can affect wildlife.

ORIENTEER

Develop a keen sense of direction and use maps to find your way through different places.

How to earn your badge
If you've qualified for the 2 star Navigation Challenge certificate of British Orienteering, you can automatically earn this badge.

Otherwise, here's what you need to do to earn this badge.
1. Learn about the map colours and common symbols used on an orienteering map.
2. Orientate a map using either terrain or a compass. Learn how to navigate while keeping the map set to the ground. 'Thumb' the map to log your changing position.
3. Complete three courses at orienteering events recognised by British Orienteering or another similar standard.
4. Show you know the safety procedures, basic first aid, appropriate clothing and equipment for countryside navigation.
5. Show that you know the Countryside Code.

PARASCENDING

Experience the thrill of parascending and do what Scouts do best – take part in everyday adventure.

How to earn your badge
1. Take part in a parascending course. Show that you can:
   - demonstrate a good landing roll
   - put on a harness and adjust it
   - assist on more than two occasions as tensiometer reader, observer or log keeper.
2. Learn the main characteristics and different types of parachutes used by parascenders.
3. Show a basic knowledge of the theory of flight.
4. Experience at least four parascending flights.

PHOTOGRAPHER

Scouts get involved in fantastic experiences. Wouldn't it be great to be able to capture them all through photography? Work towards your Photographer badge and produce stunning snapshots.

How to earn your badge
Choose one of these two options. Then complete all tasks for your chosen option.

Option 1: still photography
1. Choose one of these two activities:
   - Produce 12 photographs, featuring at least two of these photographic techniques: portrait, still life (or similar), landscape or seascape, sport or action, or timelapse.
   - Produce six black and white photographs, based on a theme of your choice. Explain the steps you took to create them and the impact of using black and white as an alternative to colour images. You could produce high quality prints on photographic paper or present them on screen.

2. Show that you know the main settings on a digital camera or a smartphone camera. This should include focus and exposure control, and flash settings. Explain the impact of shutter speed and aperture size on the image.
3. Describe what accessories are available to use with digital cameras or smartphone cameras.
4. Edit a selection of your images, using editing software on a computer or using an app on a smartphone. This could include cropping, colour, contrast or light levels. Explain what you have changed and how it improved your image.
5. Diagnose typical faults that happen at the photographing or editing stages, such as over or under exposure and high or low contrast. Explain how to reduce camera shake and how to respond to subject movement.
6. Show that you know how to care for a digital camera or smartphone camera.

Option 2: video photography
1. Produce at least two short films from two of these categories:
   - documentary
   - music video
   - drama
   - comedy
   - advertisement
   - training film.

Create a storyboard and script for each of these. Edit the film using editing software on a computer or a smartphone app.

2. Show that you understand:
   - camera techniques such as panning, zooming, close-ups, long shots and using additional lighting.
   - production techniques such as editing, how to avoid jumpy cuts and maintaining continuity.
3. Choose one of these two activities:
   - Show that you know how to care for a video camera and accessories, such as storage media, batteries, microphones and lights.
   - Discuss the differences between recording video on a video camera, digital camera and a smartphone.

Top tips
If you're doing option 2, you can complete number 1 as a small group with each person taking a different responsibility. You could assign roles like camera operator, director or editor.

 You must talk to your leader if you want to use social networking sites to show your photographs or videos. You'll want to discuss things like whether it's appropriate and whether you've asked permission from everyone involved.

PHYSICAL RECREATION

If you love a particular sport or physical activity and there's no specific activity badge for it, this badge is for you.

How to earn your badge
1. Regularly take part in an active sport or physical pursuit, which you haven't already gained an activity badge for. It could be a team game like rugby, football or water polo. Individual sports like tennis, running or gymnastics count too, so do pursuits like walking, yoga, ice skating or dancing.
2. Show a reasonable level of skill in your sport or pursuit. Show how you've improved over time.
3. Explain the rules or guidelines that govern the sport or pursuit you chose.
4. Show how you would prepare before taking part in your sport or pursuit. You could run through any special equipment or clothes you need and any warm-up and warm-down routines.
5. Explain how to care for the equipment you use. Explain what you should look out for when the equipment is nearing the end of its life.

Top tips

You can gain more than one Physical Recreation badge for different sports or pursuits.

Sports that you play after school or at weekends can count for number 1, although normal PE or games lessons don't.

PIONEER

With a few basic materials and a lot of skill, you can create amazing structures both fun and functional.

How to earn your badge

1. As a member of a group, take part in:
   - an indoor pioneering project, like constructing a guided missile launcher or chariot
   - an outdoor pioneering project, like building a monkey bridge, a raft or parallel runway.
2. Show the correct way to do these:
   - a whipping or safe rope sealing
   - a splice
   - coiling and storing a rope
   - using levers to extract objects or move heavy weights
   - being safe in pioneering projects. Explain why it's important.
3. Name and tie at least six knots and three lashings that are useful in pioneering.

POWER COXSWAIN

Master the waterways on your chosen craft and have fun while you're doing it.

How to earn your badge
If you hold The Scout Association's Personal or Leadership Activity Permit for Power Boating or Personal Watercraft (Jet Ski), a Leadership Permit for Narrow Boating or Motor Cruising or the RYA Level 1 Powerboat Award, you automatically gain this badge.

You can complete the steps using a powerboat, narrow boat, motor cruiser or on a personal watercraft.

If not, here's what you need to do.
1. Choose and identify the boat you will use.
2. Choose the waters you will visit.
3. Identify the features and hazards of this water.
4. Learn what the rules are for boating on the water you're using.
5. Wear the proper clothing and make sure you have the correct equipment for your craft.

Complete the following steps under proper supervision:

1. Locate the engine and know how to start and stop safely.
2. Take part in a man overboard drill.
3. Launch and recover your craft (if that's possible) and come alongside. Moor and berth your craft.
4. Control the speed and direction of your craft to steer around a course or on a journey.

> ❗ You must be appropriately supervised by an activity permit holder or a qualified external instructor. You must follow the activity rules in the Policy and Organisation Rules. Find out more at **scouts.org.uk/a-z**

PULLING (FIXED SEAT ROWING)

Take up your oars and cut through the water as you work towards this badge.

How to earn your badge
If you have completed the British Rowing Explore Rowing Programme in a fixed seat craft or gained a personal or leadership activity permit for pulling, you can automatically gain this badge.
If not, here's what you need to do.

1. Show that you understand the equipment required for the activity. As part of this:
   - point out and name the basic parts of a pulling boat
   - explain the importance of wearing appropriate clothing for various weather conditions
2. Show that you can take part in this activity safely. You should:
   - understand how to safely enter and exit the boat
   - understand the safety equipment required and how to use it
   - gain a basic knowledge of the rules of the road for your local waters
   - understand the difference between a lifejacket and a buoyancy aid, and demonstrate how to wear them correctly
   - from a boat, heave an unweighted line to land within reach of target five metres, within three attempts
   - learn the actions and safety requirements to take when being towed
   - know how to respond in an emergency
3. Carry out these manoeuvres in sequence:
   - take the boat away from a bank side mooring
   - row in a straight line for 100 metres
   - complete a figure-of-eight course
   - come alongside in your dinghy, to moor at a

ring, post, bollard or buoy, using a round turn and two half hitches

4. Complete two of these tasks:
   - scull over the stern between two points, 20 metres apart, and turn through 180 degrees
   - draw stroke over the bow
   - take a place as an oarsman, including stroke
   - give boat orders effectively, or listen to boat orders and act on them
   - as bowman, be a lookout and report hazards to the coxswain using standard maritime directions, such as starboard, port quarter and dead ahead

QUARTERMASTER

Whatever the adventure, keep the Troop well supplied by learning what it takes to be a good quartermaster.

How to earn your badge
Choose one of the two options. Then complete all tasks.

Option 1
1. Assist a Group or Troop Quartermaster for at least three months. Show ability in these areas:
   - care and storage of tents, including how to do simple repairs

- care and storage of cordage. This includes whipping, splicing, hanking, coiling and safety inspections
- safe storage and handling of fuels such as methylated spirits, paraffin, petrol and gas
- care of cooking stoves and cooking utensils, including simple repairs, cleaning and general maintenance
- convenient storage of a section's training and games equipment
- caring for and storing equipment used for adventurous activities, such as sailing gear, canoes and paddles, lifejackets and buoyancy aids, go-karts or climbing ropes.

2. Keep a simple record showing equipment issued and returned.
3. Show you understand that general tidiness is the secret of good quartermastering. Explain how you achieved this in the Troop or Group store.

Option 2

1. As equipment quartermaster, assist at a Nights Away experience for at least two days. During the experience show you're capable in at least three of these areas:
   - care and maintenance of all tentage, including the ability to do simple repairs to guy lines and fabric tears

- care and storage of all cordage. This includes whipping, splicing, hanking, coiling and safety inspections
- safe storage and handling of fuels used by the camp, such as methylated spirits, paraffin, petrol and gas
- care, maintenance and general storage of all tools such as axes, spades and saws
- care and storage of equipment used for adventurous activities, such as sailing gear, canoes and paddles, lifejackets and buoyancy aids, and climbing ropes.

2. Keep simple records, showing the equipment issued and returned.
3. Keep a portable first aid kit well stocked and maintained.
4. Choose tools to take to camp, to complete emergency repairs on equipment.
5. Show you understand that general tidiness is the secret of good quartermastering. Explain how you achieved this at the Nights Away experience.

SCIENTIST

Science is a part of everything we do. Try this badge to get creative with experiments and explore the hidden world of science behind everyday and adventurous activities.

How to earn your badge
Choose from options 1 or 2, then complete all of the tasks under your chosen option.

Option 1
1. Explore and discuss the science behind two Scouting activities or hobbies. For example, you could investigate the science behind a perfect campfire, how a kayak stays afloat and travels through the water, or how a compass or GPS device works.
2. Complete one of these:
   • Plan and complete your own experiment to explore the science behind one Scouting activity or hobby. Record your findings and explain what these mean to others. Try thinking of a question you want to answer or something you want to prove.
   • Plan and run an activity, demonstration or presentation to help others understand the science behind a Scouting activity or hobby.

Option 2

1. Plan and complete three science experiments or activities. You could try making invisible ink, creating an eruption, designing a catapult or putting together a battery. Check your plan with an adult first, then for each experiment:
   - Change something about the experiment or activity and try it again, at least once. Predict what you think will happen and find out if you were right.
   - Show that you understand the science behind your experiment or activity.

2. Find out how one of your experiments or activities links to the real world. Then, explain it to others. For example, if you made a battery, what are batteries usually made from? If you created an eruption, how similar or different is this to how volcanoes erupt?

Top tips

Ideas and resources for this badge can be found at **members.scouts.org.uk**

SPORTS ENTHUSIAST

If you follow a sport, rather than take part, you can prove your expert knowledge through this badge. You can choose anything from football or basketball to archery, motor racing or water polo.

How to earn your badge
1. Explain the rules governing your favourite sport.
2. Describe the levels of achievement within your chosen sport locally, nationally or internationally.
3. Show that you know some of the personalities, champions or other experts in your chosen sport. Explain how they might have inspired you.
4. Talk about the equipment needed for the sport.
5. Describe a recent major event, championship or landmark in the sport.
6. Explain how you follow your sport. How do you keep up to date with developments?

Top tips
You can gain more than one Sports Enthusiast badge if you follow more than one sport.

STREET SPORTS

Take up the challenge in an area that's gaining worldwide recognition. You can easily practice and master a street sport in the urban landscape and at your local, free skate parks.

How to earn your badge

1. Take part in a street sport like skateboarding, roller or in-line skating, Parkour or another street sport agreed by your leadership team.

2. Own or use equipment for a street sport. Show you can check, adjust and repair the equipment to ensure safe use.

3. Explain how to care for the equipment used and explain what you should look out for when equipment is nearing the end of its life.

4. Show that you're skilled in your chosen street sport and show how you've improved over three months. You could take part in an exhibition, public event or competition.

5. Explain the safety rules for your chosen sport including where to undertake street sports safely and responsibly.

SURVIVAL SKILLS

The Survival Skills badge is the ultimate challenge activity – giving you the skills to be self-reliant in tough conditions. Take on this badge and practice the skills to survive in the wild.

How to earn your badge

1. Show that you know:
   - basic knife or multi-tool skills, including safety and sharpening
   - first aid treatment you may need to use while on a survival event, considering you may have limited resources available
   - how to construct different kinds of shelter
   - how to build a fire and use basic lighting techniques. You should not use man-made materials such as paper or firelighters.
   - the various burning qualities of different woods
   - how to maintain hygiene in a survival situation
   - the correct use of international distress signals, using a whistle, torch, mirror or markers
   - some basic actions to take while waiting rescue that will both keep you (and your group) safe and will assist your rescuers in locating you.

2. Put together a personal survival kit.

3. With a group of at least three Scouts, take part in a survival exercise. It should last about 24 hours and the group should:

- construct a shelter of natural or salvaged materials and sleep in it
- prepare a meal using raw ingredients that could have been found or caught
- cook all meals over an open fire
- cook without utensils, although you may use a knife.

Your leadership team should select a suitable location for number 3 so that you can be supervised. Wild mountainous country is not suitable. You must also follow the rules for the Nights Away scheme.

WATER ACTIVITIES

If you like nothing more than taking to the open water – at sea or fresh water, on the water or under – then you could be eligible for this badge.

How to earn your badge
You need to reach one of these standards:
- Snorkel Diver Award of the British Sub-Aqua Club.
- British Surfing Association's Junior Scheme Level 3 Award.
- British Water Ski Federation Cutting Edge Bronze Award.
- Royal Yachting Association National (RYA) Youth Windsurfing Scheme Stage 1.
- British Sub-Aqua Club Scuba Experience or the Discover Scuba Diving Award of the Professional Association of Diving Instructors.
- BKSA (British Kite Surfing Association) Level One.

Top tips
UK Headquarters can provide alternative requirements for water sports not listed above.
You can gain a badge for every standard you meet.
This badge is for non-boating activities.
If you're interested in boating, you might prefer

Dragon Boating, Power Coxswain, Pulling or
Nautical Skills.

 Your leader must make sure you're following
the activity rules in chapter nine of the Policy,
Organisation and Rules and the Adventurous
Activity Permit Scheme.

WORLD FAITHS

Finding out about different faiths
can help you better understand
others and find common ground.

How to earn your badge
1. Complete one of these activities:
   - Visit a place of worship for a faith that you are
     not familiar with. Find out the differences
     between this building and another place
     of worship.
   - Attend a festival or event linked to a faith that
     you are not familiar with.
2. Complete one of these activities:
   - Learn about the life of a founder or a
     prominent leader of a faith. You could learn
     about people like Prince Siddhartha Gautama,
     Mohammed, Jesus Christ or a saint such as
     St George.
   - Find out about someone whose faith has had
     a significant impact upon their life.

3. Read a text from a faith that you are not familiar with. Show or discuss how this compares to your own beliefs.
4. Find out how following the teachings of a particular faith affects an individual's daily life. This could include food or dietary laws, rituals, prayer and worship, or religious observances.

Top tips
There are lots of places of worship you could visit for number 1, including a Gurdwara, Temple, Mosque, Church or Synagogue.

WRITER

Could you be the next Philip Pullman or Cressida Cowell? Maybe you'll be a prize winning journalist. Practice the craft of telling a good story through writing.

How to earn your badge
Complete four of these activities. Talk about your choice with an appropriate adult.
- Compose a poem of at least eight lines. Discuss its meaning and construction.
- Create a short story of around 600 words. Talk about your story idea with an appropriate adult beforehand.
- Write a descriptive passage of around 600

words on a subject, agreed with an appropriate adult beforehand.

- Write a 600-word review of a favourite book, play or other work of literature and talk about it with an appropriate adult.
- Produce a published article of around 600 words in length. You could contribute to a school, faith, community or Scout magazine or write a letter to a local paper.
- Keep a diary on a subject, for a length of time agreed with an appropriate adult beforehand.
- Write a play or dramatic sketch lasting at least 10 minutes.
- Interview a local celebrity, or other notable person. Write or type out the interview to show the questions you asked and the interviewee's replies.
- Write a letter to a pen pal (real or imaginary) of at least 600 words.

ACTIVITY PLUS

Do you want to take your skills in an activity even further? If you've achieved the highest level of any of the badges in this book, and you want to get better at your chosen activity, the Activity Plus badges could be your next big challenge.

Your Leader can award it if you demonstrate significant achievement in an activity. You Leader can also award you if you've gone above and beyond your own abilities, or you've taken something on even though you don't have the best facilities available.

To earn an Activity Plus badge you need to:
- hold your chosen activity badge
- agree a target with your Leader before attempting the Activity Plus badge. It may involve you taking part in additional training or practice to develop your knowledge or skills further.
- demonstrate to your leader that you have met your target.

Here are a few examples of targets for Scouts:
- For the Pulling (Fixed Seat Rowing) PLUS, take charge of a boat under oars.

- For the Meteorologist PLUS, keep a weather diary for an agreed number of months.
- For the Dragon Boating PLUS, train for a month as part of a team to compete in a national dragon boating competition.
- For the Paddle Sports PLUS, gain the British Canoeing Paddle Power Explore levels 8 and 9, or the British Canoeing Paddle Power Excel.
- For relevant PLUS badges, gain a personal or leadership permit, or an NGB qualification for the activity.

The only activities that **are not included** in the Activity Plus are Athletics, Athletics Plus, Community Impact, Hikes Away, Nights Away and Time on Water. For staged activities, you can only be awarded and Activity Plus badge if you've completed the highest stage.

INSTRUCTOR

If you want to pass your skills on to others, why not take the Instructor badge? They can be achieved for almost all activity badges in the Scouts.

Here's what you need to do to earn this badge.
1. Hold the activity badge in your chosen activity.
2. Know what a Scout has to do to achieve the activity badge, so that you can instruct them in that subject.
3. Attend a training course covering the technical skills involved in the activity badge and the use of appropriate training methods. If there's no recognised technical skill course for your badge, an individual training programme can be arranged with a qualified instructor.
4. Assist with the training of Scouts in the subject, over a period of at least three months.

Top tips
You need to do 1, 2 and 3 before you can begin number 4.
If you already have an Instructor badge in another area, you may not have to complete number 3.

STAGED ACTIVITY BADGES

BE DETERMINED...

Staged activity badges

Staged activity badges give you the chance to try something new or get better at something you already know.

Choosing the right stage for you – whether it's stage 1, 2 or more – isn't about your age. It depends on the experience or skills you already have in that area. You can jump ahead to a higher stage if you're ready or start at the beginning to build up skills and knowledge as you work gradually through the stages.

Talk to your leader about what's best for you.

AIR ACTIVITIES

Explore the secrets and the science of flight. You'll learn about the workings of aircraft, how to chart a journey across the sky and how to prototype your own flying machine.

Now, get ready for take-off...

Air Activities – stage 1
How to earn your badge

1. Make an aircraft out of paper and see how well it flies. You could use a paper dart or a helicopter and drop it from a height.
2. Find out about one kind of aircraft and tell others in your section about it. It could be a commercial aircraft like Concorde or Airbus or a military aircraft like a Spitfire, Lynx or Chinook.
3. Spell your name using the phonetic alphabet.
4. Talk to somebody who has flown in an aircraft, helicopter or hot air balloon. What was it like? If you have already flown in an aircraft, tell others in your section about it.
5. Tell others in your section about an aircraft (real or imagined) that you would like to fly in and why. You can do this through drawings or models.

Air Activities – stage 2
How to earn your badge
1. Make and fly a model aeroplane, three different types of paper glider, a hot air balloon or a kite.
2. Choose 3 of these:
   - Name and identify the main parts of an aeroplane
   - Identify six airlines from their markings.
   - Name and identify different types of aircraft (such as powered aeroplanes, airships, gliders or unmanned aircraft)
   - Collect and identify six pictures of different aircraft. Share them with others in your section.
   - Explain how different weather conditions can affect air activities.
   - Fly in an aircraft and tell the rest of your section about it.
   - Meet someone who flies regularly and talk to them about their experiences.
3. Send a simple message using the phonetic alphabet.
4. Visit an airfield, air display or air museum.
5. Know the dangers involved in visiting an airfield.

Air Activities – stage 3
How to earn your badge

1. Construct and fly a chuck glider for at least five seconds. You can also build and fly a miniature hot air balloon or kite instead.

2. Understand the terms nose, fuselage, tail, wings, port, starboard and tailfin. Learn the names of an aeroplane's control surfaces.

3. Choose one of these activities:
   - Collect photographs or pictures of six aircraft that interest you. Name them and identify their operational uses.
   - Tell others about an airline that you are interested in, or have travelled on, including the airline's uniform and logos.
   - Find out about unmanned aircraft, such as drones, and the rules around flying them safely.

4. Show how you would get a weather forecast for an air activity.

5. Send and receive a simple message using the phonetic alphabet. Explain why it is used in aviation.

6. Draw a diagram or make a model of an airfield to show and name different points. Use your diagram model to explain the rules for access to an airfield.

7. Take part in a visit to a place of aviation interest, such as an airfield, air display or air museum. Tell others about something you learnt.

8. Using 1:50000 and 1:25000 OS maps, show you understand the meaning of scale and common map symbols. Explain how a pilot might use a map differently from a car driver or somebody on a hike
9. Use a flight simulator programme. Show the effects of the controls.

Air Activities – stage 4
How to earn your badge
1. Trim a paper aeroplane or model glider to perform a straight glide, stall and turn.
2. Name the main control surfaces of an aeroplane and how they work.
3. Identify six aircraft in use today from pictures or in flight. At least two of the six must be civil commercial aircraft, one must be a military aircraft and another two must be light private aircraft.
4. Explain how wind speed and direction are measured. How does the weather affect air activities?
5. Explain the difference between a Mayday radio call and a Pan-Pan radio call. Give examples of when each might be used.
6. Choose one of these activities:
   • Help to organise a visit to an airfield or place of aviation history for a group of Scouts (Beavers, Cubs, Scouts or Explorers). Explain what the Scouts will need to know before the visit.

- Take part in a flight (for example in a light aircraft or glider) as a passenger.
7. Draw a runway and its circuit patterns.
8. Learn the common types of charts and the conventional signs used on them
9. Show how to perform a pre-flight check on a light aircraft, microlight or glider. Explain why inspecting each part is important.
10. Show how to do a take-off and landing using a flight simulator computer programme that uses a joystick.

Air Activities – stage 5
How to earn your badge
1. Build a scale model from a plastic kit, plans or photographs.
2. Explain the relationship between lift, drag, thrust and weight.
3. Choose one of these activities:
   - Explain the basic principles of a piston engine, including the four-stroke cycle, with consideration of valve and ignition timing.
   - Explain the similarities and differences between a piston engine and a jet engine, covering the main parts and workings
4. Explain how wind direction and strength is important in take-off and landing. Explain how a wing gives lift and why a wing stalls.
5. Explain how temperature and atmospheric pressure are measured in weather forecasting.

6. Explain basic cloud types, how they are formed and why they're relevant to air activities.

7. Tell others about the duties of either:
- an aircraft marshaller, demonstrating marshalling signals
- a crew leader for a glider launch. Show their procedure and the signals they use.

8. Imagine you're planning a cross-country flight of at least 60 nautical miles, at an air speed of 90 knots. What would the time of flight be, from an overhead starting point to another overhead destination? Your assessor will give you a head or tail wind to factor in when you're working this out.

9. Take part in a flight (for example in a light aircraft or glider) and point out the landmarks that you fly over on an aviation chart

10. Explain the purpose of a pre-flight checklist and the main items you would check.

11. Find out about the different types of air traffic control services used at airfields and airports. Explain how this would be different at a small local airfield compared to a large international airport.

Air Activities – stage 6
How to earn your badge

1. Build and fly (from plans, kits or from scratch) one of these:
   - rubber band powered model aircraft for 15 seconds
   - glider for 15 seconds
   - model airship
   - hovercraft
   - round the pole model (RTP).
2. Explain what trim is and the importance of weight and balance.
3. Explain why flaps, slots and slats can be found on aircraft and how they work. Give examples of aircraft that use these devices.
4. Identify the weather conditions associated with the movement of air masses over the UK, such as tropical, maritime and continental.
5. Interpret Met Office reports and forecasts for pilots including METAR and TAF.
6. Find out why Morse code is still transmitted by navigational beacons. Recognise six three-letter sequences.
7. Identify:
   - runway and airfield markings
   - light and pyrotechnics signals
8. Find out the reasons for civilian airport security, the main threats and ways of counteracting them.

9. Explain how an aircraft compass and a direction indicator works, as well as potential errors.
10. Explain how aircraft pressure instruments, altimeters and airspeed indicators work.
11. Take an active part in at least three flights. Show how you develop your skills with each flight, including assisting with navigation and flight planning, and learning how controlled airspace might affect these flights.
12. Tell others about the emergency procedures for one type of aircraft such as a powered light aircraft, microlight, glider or small helicopter. What should be done in the event of engine failure, cable break or autorotation?

COMMUNITY IMPACT

Making a difference in the world is such an important part of being a Scout. The Community Impact staged activities give you the chance to make the most of your time, create positive social change, help people in your community and make the world a better place.

Top tips
The Community Impact staged activities play a really important part in Scouting, so we've put together some special guidance for leaders so they can help and encourage you to complete the activities. You can find this on page 221.

You can contact your councillor, Member of Parliament (UK), Assembly Member (Wales), Member of the Scottish Parliament (Scotland) or Member of the Legislative Assembly (Northern Ireland) using **theyworkforyou.com** or **writetothem.com**

You'll find voluntary organisations who want to support young people in community impact projects on **stepuptoserve.org.uk**

Community Impact – stage 1
How to earn your badge

1. **Identify need.** Investigate what issues and challenges exist in your chosen community – it could be local, national or international.

2. **Plan action.** Decide what issue your section should take action on and what you want to change. Talk to your section about what actions you would like to take.

3. **Take action over three months.** You should:
   - spend at least fours hours personally taking action on your chosen issue. You can achieve more impact by spreading your time out over a month, instead of doing it all in one go.
   - involve others in the action. Work in a team with your section and preferably people in the community you are trying to help.

4. **Learn and make more change.** Discuss what you've learned with your section. Talk about how you have made people's lives better, what you could do to help more people in your chosen community and how taking action has developed you.

5. **Tell the world.** Help other people to understand why the issue you took action on is important, what you did and how they can help.

Community Impact – stage 2
How to earn your badge

1. **Identify need.** Investigate what issues and challenges exist in your chosen community – it could be local, national or international.

2. **Plan action.** Decide what issue your section would like to take action on and what you would like to change. Work with a group of people not involved in Scouting, who are passionate about your cause, to plan action that will make a positive difference.

3. **Take action over six months.** You should:
    - spend at least 12 hours personally taking action on your chosen issue. You can achieve more impact by spreading your time out, over four months, instead of doing it all in one go.
    - involve others in the action. Work in a team with your section and preferably people in the community you are trying to help.

4. **Learn and make more change:** Discuss with your section what you've learned, how you have made people's lives better and what you could do to help even more people in your chosen community.

5. **Tell the world**. Help other people to understand the issue you have made a positive impact on is important and why it's important. Show what you did and how they can also help.

Community Impact – stage 3
How to earn your badge

1. **Identify need.** Investigate what issues and challenges exist in your chosen community – local, national or international.

2. **Plan action.** Decide what issue your section would like to take action on and what you would like to change. Work with a group of people not involved in Scouting, who are passionate about your cause, to plan action that will make a positive difference.

3. **Take action over nine months.** You should:
   - spend at least 24 hours in total personally taking action on your chosen issue. You can achieve more impact by spreading your time out, over six months, instead of doing it all in one go.
   - involve others from your section and a group of non-Scouts, preferably from the community you are trying to help.

4. **Learn and make more change.** Talk about what you learned with your section, how you have made people's lives better and what you could do to help more people in your chosen community.

5. **Tell the world.** Help other people to understand why your chosen issue is important, what you did and how they can also help.

Community Impact – stage 4
How to earn your badge

1. **Identify need.** Find out what issues and challenges exist in your chosen community – locally, nationally or internationally.

2. **Plan action.** Decide what issue your section would like to take action – what do you want to change? Work with a group of people who are not involved in Scouting, and are passionate about your cause, to plan action that will make a positive difference.

3. **Take action over 12 months.** You should:
   - spend at least 48 hours personally taking action on your chosen issue. You can achieve more impact by spreading your time out over the year, instead of doing it all in one go.
   - involve your section and a group of non-Scouts, preferably people from the community you are trying to help.

4. **Learn and make more change.** Talk about what you learned with your section, how you have made people's lives better and what you could do to help more people in your chosen community.

5. **Tell the world.** Help other people to understand why your chosen issue is important, how you have made a positive impact and how they can help.

DIGITAL CITIZEN

The digital world is part of our
everyday lives. It helps us reach
other people, learn new things
and explore the world at the
touch of a button. When you know how to use the
tools available to you, the possibilities are endless.

Take the digital citizen badge and develop the
knowledge you need in all things digital.

❗ There are rules and guidance around staying
safe online that your Leader will need to make
sure you're aware of – whichever stage you're
going for. See page 225 to find out more.

Digital Citizen – stage 1
How to earn your badge
Complete every task to achieve Stage 1, showing
that you have thought about the potential risks and
how to stay safe for each activity.
1. In a creative way of your choice, map out your
   regular digital actions, such as searches, clicks or
   posts.
   • Discuss with other young people the
     information you leave behind as a result of
     these digital actions, and whether that's OK
     or not.

2. Learn how to create a secure password and make one of your own.
   - Always do this with a trusted adult.
3. Share three ways young people can respond positively when someone's being unkind or dishonest, including telling an adult if someone's making you feel uncomfortable.
4. Use an online service to learn a new skill and show others what you've learnt.

Digital Citizen – stage 2
How to earn your badge
Complete every task to achieve Stage 2, showing that you have thought about the potential risks and how to stay safe for each activity.

1. Create a list of rights that you think you should have as a young person when online.
   - Find online examples of where you think these rights are respected.
2. For a week, keep track of how much time you spend online and what you're doing.
   - send or reply to someone with a short email Looking back over the week, discuss with someone if you're happy with how you spent your time or not.
3. Show that you can spot the difference between facts and opinions posted online.

4. Investigate how people from different backgrounds interact online.
   - Share how you'd act differently because of these differences. People might be from different countries, be different ages, have different abilities or amounts of money, etc.
5. In a team, learn about a topic you care about and share with others what you've learnt.
   - You must use a mixture of online and offline tools, and discuss which you preferred and why.

Digital Citizen – stage 3
How to earn your badge
Complete every task to achieve Stage 4, showing that you have thought about the potential risks and how to stay safe for each activity.

1. In a creative way of your choice, map out what digital actions other people take which makes information about you public.
   - Discuss with other young people what the positive and negative consequences of this might be, and what actions you can take to protect yourself.
2. Create something that helps other young people to know what they should do if they're made to feel uncomfortable online, and where they can find support.

3. Investigate if the people you interact with most online are similar to you, or different to you (ie what are their ages, genders, ethnicities, hobbies etc?).
   - What impact might that have on the views and opinions you see and believe?
4. Use several online services to research a personal opportunity that excites you but you know little about (such as a new hobby, studying at college or university, or a specific career).
5. In a team, use a digital collaboration tool of your choice to achieve one of the following:
   - Something that benefits your Scout Group.
   - Something that benefits a local charity.
   - Something that promotes young people's voices to local decision makers.

Digital Citizen – stage 4
How to earn your badge
Complete every task to achieve Stage 4, showing that you have thought about the potential risks and how to stay safe for each activity.
1. Show that you understand your rights regarding online information by completing one of the following:
   - In a creative way of your choice, show all the information someone could find about you online and how you'd hide that information if

you wanted to. Leave out anything you're uncomfortable with.

- Research different ways in which your personal information can be used by algorithms or targeted advertising, and create an activity to show other young people what you found out.

2. Take part in a debate on a topic that you think there may be lots of misinformation about online.
   - Use evidence you've found online only. After the debate, discuss how easy it was to know if the evidence you found was reliable or not

3. Create a digital version of the Scout Law which shows how each law can be followed when online.

4. Complete an online training course of your choice and share some of what you learned with other young people.

5. In a team that includes young people from other parts of the country or world, use a digital collaboration tool of your choice to achieve one of the following:
   - Something that benefits Scouts.
   - Something that benefits a charity or cause you all care about.
   - Something that promotes young people's voices within national decision makers.

DIGITAL MAKER

Digital skills can be used to solve problems, build resilience, help communities and inspire creativity.

Remember – if you already know a bit about developing, you can skip to the stage that matches your ability.

Top tips
For stages 1 and 2 the only technology you need is a laptop. If you don't have access to Wifi in your meeting place, you can still achieve this badge with just a bit of preparation.

Digital Maker – stage 1
In stage 1 you will learn what digital making is and how it fits with Scouting and the wider world.

How to earn your badge
1. Show that you know what a computer is and understand that there are lots of uses for digital technology in everyday life. Think about where you see computer systems and technology in your day-to-day life, and about how digital technology helps make things better or easier.
2. Create a graphic for a computer game, app, or website. This could be a background scene, character, or other image.

3. Write clear instructions for a computer or person to follow to complete a task.

For top tips, resources and activities, visit
scouts.org.uk/digitalmaker

Digital Maker – stage 2
In stage 2 you will demonstrate that you can complete digital projects which can be used in Scouting activities or in the wider world.

How to earn your badge
1. Create a piece of interactive or animated digital art using software.
2. Create a simple computer program to help with a scouting activity, and try it out.
3. Make a simple digital creation that uses code to interact with the wider world through inputs (such as buttons or typing on a keyboard) and outputs (such as a computer screen, sound, or lights).

For top tips, resources and activities, visit
scouts.org.uk/digitalmaker

Digital Maker – stage 3
In stage 3 you will demonstrate that you can use and combine a variety of digital making skills to complete projects that can be used in Scouting activities or in the wider world.

How to earn your badge

1. In a coding language of your choice, create a basic program to meet a need of Scouting or your section.
2. Use a programmable device (such as Arduino, Raspberry Pi, or micro:bit) with electronic components, code, and appropriate materials to create an electronic gadget and use it in a Scouting activity.
3. Design and create digital graphics for use as part of one of the above. The elements of the project should all fit within the project's specific purpose.
4. Show and present your digital making project, explaining the challenges that you encountered while creating it and how you addressed them.

For top tips and guidance visit
scouts.org.uk/digitalmaker

Digital Maker – stage 4
In stage 4 you will demonstrate that you can combine a variety of digital making skills to solve a problem or meet a challenge related to Scouting.

How to earn your badge

1. Using a combination of programming, digital art, digital devices, electronic components, and other appropriate materials, create something that could serve a purpose in a Scouting activity.

2. Attend a digital making event and show your work, or help somebody else in your section or another section to work towards a Digital Maker Staged Activity badge.

For top tips and guidance for leaders visit
scouts.org.uk/digitalmaker

Digital Maker – stage 5
In stage 5, you will combine your digital making skills to identify and solve a real problem in the local or global community. You will go through the process of project design from concept, to testing and implementation, and finally to sharing your new knowledge with others.

How to earn your badge
1. Identify a real-life local or global problem and design, build, test, and improve a solution by combining your digital making skills and selecting appropriate software tools, digital devices, components, and materials.
2. Create and share a resource that would allow someone else to replicate your project with minimal previous knowledge. This resource should be digital, and it can be any format you like: a video (or a series!), an online (printable) document, an entry on a tutorials website such as Instructables, a blog post. Or meet with people

who could benefit from your solution to share how you created it and explain how it can help them.

For top tips and guidance for leaders visit
scouts.org.uk/digitalmaker

EMERGENCY AID

When accidents cause someone to get hurt, it can make a huge difference if there's someone on the scene who knows what to do.

Learn how to help in emergency situations by working through your Emergency Aid staged activities. It'll help you develop you skills in supporting others and caring for yourself.

Emergency Aid – stage 1
How to earn your badge
Show you understand all of the actions listed.

Explain to your leader or another adult about:
- the importance of getting help
- what to say when you call 999
- helping someone who is unconscious
- helping someone who is bleeding
- reassuring someone at the scene of an emergency.

Emergency Aid – stage 2
How to earn your badge
Show you understand all of the actions listed under each number.

1. Explain to your leader or another adult about:
   - the importance of getting help
   - what to say when you call 999
   - reassuring someone at the scene of an emergency.
2. Explain how to help someone who:
   - is unconscious
   - is bleeding
   - has a burn
   - is having an asthma attack.

If you hold a first aid award covering this or a similar syllabus from a recognised first aid provider (such as the British Red Cross or St John Ambulance) you can automatically get this badge.

Emergency Aid – stage 3
How to earn your badge
You will need to take part in around two to three hours of training, which should be taught by an adult with relevant knowledge.

1. Explain to your leader or another adult about how to call 999.
2. Explain how you help someone who:
   - is unconscious
   - is unconscious and not breathing
   - is bleeding
   - has a burn
   - has heat exhaustion

- has hypothermia
- is choking.

If you hold a first aid award covering this or a similar syllabus from a recognised first aid provider (such as the British Red Cross or St John Ambulance) you can automatically get this badge.

Emergency Aid – stage 4
How to earn your badge
You will need to take part in around three to six hours of training, which should be taught by an adult with relevant knowledge.

1. Explain to your leader or another adult about how to call 999.
2. Explain how you help someone who:
   - is unconscious
   - is unconscious and not breathing
   - is bleeding
   - has a burn
   - has heat exhaustion
   - has hypothermia
   - is choking
   - is having an asthma attack
   - is having a heart attack
   - has a head injury
   - has a suspected spinal injury
   - has a broken bone

- has a sprain or strain
- has meningitis.

If you hold a first aid award covering this or a similar syllabus from a recognised first aid provider (such as the British Red Cross or St John Ambulance) you can automatically get this badge.

You must take part in formal training to gain this badge – a first aid award covering this or a similar syllabus. Your training must be from a recognised first aid provider, such as the British Red Cross or St Johns Ambulance, or someone qualified to deliver First Response.

Emergency Aid – stage 5
How to earn your badge
You will need to take part in around six to eight hours of training, which should be taught by an adult with relevant knowledge.

1. Explain to your leader or another adult about how to call 999.
2. Explain how you help someone who:
   - is unconscious
   - is unconscious and not breathing
   - is bleeding
   - has a burn
   - has heat exhaustion
   - has hypothermia

- is choking
- is having an asthma attack
- is having a heart attack
- has a head injury
- has a suspected spinal injury
- has a broken bone
- has a sprain or strain
- has meningitis
- is having a stroke
- is experiencing a diabetic emergency
- is having a severe allergic reaction
- is having a seizure.

If you hold a first aid award covering this or a similar syllabus from a recognised first aid provider (such as the British Red Cross or St John Ambulance) you can automatically get this badge.

You must take part in formal training to gain this badge – a first aid award covering this or a similar syllabus. Your training must be from a recognised first aid provider, such as the British Red Cross or St Johns Ambulance.

HIKES AWAY

Your first hike away is an amazing milestone, which deserves to be recognised. And as you become more experienced in hikes away, you can pick up other badges.

How to earn your badges
There are eight different badges you can collect. Each one marks a certain number of hikes or journeys you will have completed:

1   2   5   10   15   20   35   50

Each hike or journey must involve at least four hours of activity and have a purpose, which you will agree with your leader. The sorts of activity that count as a hike away include:

- taking part in a dusk to dawn hike
- exploring a bridleway on horseback
- an overnight expedition by foot
- a trip down a river in an open canoe
- a cycle ride
- any other similar activity.

Be dressed and equipped for the weather conditions and terrain. Your leader will also need to make sure you're following the rules in chapter nine of the Policy and Organisation Rules and the Activity Permit Scheme.

MUSICIAN

A piano playing maestro, a guitar hero or singing sensation – whatever you want to be, practice and perform as a musician with these great activities.

Musician – stage 1
How to earn your badge

1. **Skill**
   - Listen to a short tune of a couple of lines and then sing it back.
   - Listen to another tune and then beat or clap out the rhythm.
2. **Performance** Sing or play two different types of song or tune on your chosen instrument – remember your voice is an instrument too. You must perform in front of other people, either in Scouting or at a public performance such as a group show or school concert.
3. **Knowledge**
   - Demonstrate some of the musical exercises that you use to practice your skills.
   - Talk about your instrument and why you enjoy playing it. Alternatively, you could talk about the songs you sing and why you enjoy singing them.
4. **Interest** Tell your assessor about the music that you most like to listen to.

Musician – stage 2
How to earn your badge

1. **Skill** Reach Grade One standard for the Associated Board of the Royal School of Music (or similar).It can be on an instrument of your choice orby singing.

2. **Performance** Sing or play two different types of song or tune on your chosen instrument. You must perform in front of other people either in Scouting or at a public performance.

3. **Knowledge** Demonstrate some of the musical exercises that you use to practice your skills.
   - Talk about your instrument and why you enjoy playing it. Alternatively, you could talk about the songs you sing and why you enjoy singing them.
   - Name a piece of music associated with your instrument.
   - Name several musicians who you have heard.

4. **Interest** Talk about your own interests in music, including what you listen to most and how it's similar or different to the music you play or sing.

Musician – stage 3
How to earn your badge

1. **Skill** Reach Grade Two standard for the Associated Board of the Royal School of Music (or similar).It can be on an instrument of your choice or by singing.

2. **Performance** Sing or play, as a solo or with others, two different types of song or tune on your chosen instrument. You must perform in front of other people, either in Scouting or at a public performance such as a group show or school concert.

3. **Knowledge**
   - Demonstrate some of the musical exercises that you use to practice your skills.
   - Talk about your instrument and why you enjoy playing it. Alternatively, talk about the songs you sing and why you enjoy singing them.
   - Talk about three well known pieces of music associated with your instrument or chosen songs.

4. **Interest** Talk about your own interests in music, including what you listen to most and how this is similar to or different from the music you play or sing.

Musician – stage 4
How to earn your badge
1. **Skill** Reach Grade Three standard for the Associated Board of the Royal School of Music (or similar).
    It can be on an instrument of your choice or by singing.
2. **Performance** Sing or play three different types of song or tune on your chosen instrument. One should be a solo and one should be played with other musicians in an arrangement of your choice. Your performance should be public, such as at a Group show, school concert or church service.
3. **Knowledge**
    - Demonstrate some of the musical exercises that you use to practice your skills.
    - Talk about your instrument and why you enjoy playing it. Alternatively, talk about the songs you sing and why you enjoy singing them.
    - Talk about some of the musicians who are associated with your instrument.
4. **Interest** Talk about your own interests in music, including what you listen to most and how it's similar or different to the music you play or sing.

Musician – stage 5
How to earn your badge

1. **Skill** Reach Grade Five standard for the Associated Board of the Royal School of Music (or similar) on the instrument of your choice or by singing.

2. **Performance** Sing or play three different types of song or tune on your chosen instrument. One should be a solo and one should be played with other musicians in an arrangement of your choice. Your performance should be public such as at a group show or church service.

3. **Knowledge**
   - Demonstrate some of the musical exercises that you use to practice your skills.
   - Talk about your instrument and why you enjoy playing it. Alternatively, talk about the songs you sing and why you enjoy singing them.
   - Name several well known pieces of music associated with your instrument.
   - Name several musicians associated with your instrument.

4. **Interest** Talk about your own interests in music, including what you listen to most and how it's similar or different to the music you play or sing.

NAUTICAL SKILLS

Unleash your inner seafarer and
develop the skills to take a boat
or other craft out on the open water.

Nautical Skills – stage 1
How to earn your badge
1. Take part in a water activity taster session.
   You could try:
   - paddle sports
   - rafting
   - sailing
   - windsurfing
   - pulling.
2. Correctly identify the different equipment used
   for the activity you chose.
3. Gain an understanding of the safety
   equipment used.

Nautical Skills – stage 2
How to earn your badge
1. Take part in a water activity taster session for at
   least one hour. By the end of the session you
   should be comfortable in your craft. You could try:
   - paddle sports
   - rafting
   - sailing
   - windsurfing
   - pulling.

2. Show that you understand what to do in the event of a capsize or man overboard situation in your chosen activity.
3. Demonstrate that you can tie either a figure of eight or a reef knot. Describe how you use them in water activities.
4. Name the basic equipment you used during your chosen activity.
5. List some clothing that is not suitable for your chosen activity, and explain the reasons why.
6. Show that you know the safety equipment you used and why it's needed.

Nautical Skills – stage 3
How to earn your badge
1. Take part in at least two one-hour taster sessions in two different water based activities. By the end of the session you should be competent at controlling your craft. You could try:
   - canoeing
   - a powered activity like yachting
   - pulling
   - sailing
   - windsurfing.
2. Show that you know how to act safely in your chosen activity if you are involved in a capsize or man overboard situation.

3. Show how to check water depth using a method appropriate to your activity so that you don't ground or beach.
4. Show how to tie a clove hitch, a bowline knot, and a round turn and two half-hitches. Explain when these would be used.
5. Name the parts of one type of watercraft.
6. Demonstrate and explain what clothing is suitable for the activities used in your chosen activity.
7. Explain the basic safety rules that apply to your chosen activity.
8. Explain the difference between a buoyancy aid and a life jacket, when each should be used and how they function. Show how they are worn.

Nautical Skills – stage 4
How to earn your badge
1. Develop your skills in two water based activities. Show competency and technique in:
   - launch and recovering a watercraft
   - manoeuvring a watercraft
   - communicating with the group
   - knowledge of safety.
2. Take part in a capsize and recovery drill for the two watercraft you have chosen.
3. Use a throw bag or line to reach a person six metres away in the water.

4. Show you know how to apply the steering rules to your chosen watercraft and recognise the main channel markers.
5. Use a knot (either a round turn and two half hitches or a bowline) or a cleat correctly to moor a boat with a painter or mooring line. Describe what you need to be aware of when using these to moor.
6. Complete one of the following:
   - Pipe the 'still' and 'carry on' on a Bosun's call.
   - Make a sail maker's whipping and one other type of whipping and safely heat-seal the end of a rope. Describe the correct use of these whippings.
   - Make an eye splice or a back splice and safely heat-seal the end of a rope. Describe the correct use of these splices.
7. Name the parts of your chosen watercraft. If you have completed Nautical Skills Stage 3 you must choose a different watercraft.
8. Take part in a challenging three-hour expedition or exercise afloat.
9. Take part in a competition or crew-based activity in your chosen watercraft.

Nautical Skills – stage 5
How to earn your badge
1. Develop your skills in one water based activity to a level where you can operate the watercraft safely. You could demonstrate this by gaining a

personal permit or the relevant national governing body personal competency award.

2. Show how you would use your watercraft to recover others from the water by taking part in a simple rescue exercise.

3. Demonstrate knowledge of pilotage, navigation lights, sound signals, tides, currents and eddies, depending on what's relevant to your local waterways.

4. Demonstrate that you can tie a figure-of-eight knot, clove hitch, and a round turn and two half-hitches. Tie an additional three knots: sheet bend, rolling hitch and bowline, then describe their uses.

5. Explain the different types of ropes used in water activities, their advantages and disadvantages and how to care for them.

6. Complete one of these:
   - Make a rope fender or other piece of decorative rope work, such as a lanyard or a decorative knot.
   - Demonstrate three calls made on a Bosun's pipe, other than 'still' and 'carry on'.
   - Hoist the colours for a Sea Scout ceremonial or nautical themed ceremony.

7. Plan and take part in a one-day expedition or exercise afloat with others.

8. Learn how different boats communicate with each other in your location.

9. Take on the helm or cox role in a watercraft or help prepare a team for a competition.
10. Learn how to get local weather forecasts, understand their importance and be able to recognise signs of changing weather.
11. Learn how to safeguard against the effects of cold, and how to recognise and treat hypothermia.

Nautical Skills – stage 6
How to earn your badge

1. Develop your skills in one water based activity to a level where you can operate the watercraft safely. You could demonstrate this by gaining a personal permit. If you have completed Nautical Skills Stage 5, you should try a different water based activity.
2. Learn about flares, distress signals and marine VHF radio, and when it is appropriate to use them.
3. Learn about and explain the access and mooring issues in your chosen activity.
4. Learn about and explain the 'nautical rules of the road' including passing other watercraft, the International Rules for Preventing Collisions at Sea (IRPCS), light signals, sound signals and the use of channels.
5. Show an understanding of the maintenance your watercraft needs and show you can carry out simple repairs over the course of three months.

6. Plan and take part in an overnight expedition by water with others. Your time underway should be at least six hours.

NAVIGATOR

Lead your team, take charge and set the course for an adventure. With your keen sense of direction and your Navigator staged activity badge, you need never lose your way.

Navigator – stage 1
How to earn your badge

1. Locate yourself on a simple map. You could use a map of a local park, nature reserve, zoo, or even a theme park.
2. Identify a number of features or locations on that map. You could pinpoint locations like the toilets, car park, bird hide or picnic area.
3. Learn the four cardinal points of a compass.
4. Draw a simple map of where you live, your meeting place or another area local to you.
5. Use a map during an outdoor activity.
6. Show you understand how to dress appropriately and what equipment you and the adults will need on the activity.

Navigator – stage 2
How to earn your badge
1. Learn how to read a four-figure grid reference.
2. Understand how to use the key of a map.
3. Use a map during an outdoor activity.
4. Draw a simple map to direct someone from your meeting place to a local point of interest.
5. With other Scouts, go for a walk with a leader around the local area. Take it in turns to use one of these methods of navigation:
   - written instructions
   - recorded instructions
   - road signs
   - tracking signs
   - maps.
6. Learn the eight points of a compass and use them in an activity.
7. Show you know how to dress appropriately for the activities involved in this badge and what equipment you and the adults need on the activities.

Navigator – stage 3
How to earn your badge
1. Learn how to read a six figure grid reference.
2. Understand contour lines on an Ordnance Survey map.

3. Using 1:50000 and 1:25000 scale Ordnance Survey maps show that you understand the meaning of scale, can set the map to north and can recognise conventional map symbols.
4. Follow and walk a route of at least 5km, using a map to navigate for at least part of the journey. Your Leader can plan the route but you'll work with other Scouts, or take turns, to navigate.
5. Show you know how to dress appropriately and what kit you and your group will need.

Navigator – stage 4
How to earn your badge
1. Show you know how to:
   - convert grid bearings to magnetic bearings and vice versa
   - use back bearings to check the route
   - estimate your current position using a compass
   - walk on a bearing, including 'deviating from course' (the four right angles technique to bypass an obstacle)
   - read a six figure grid reference.
2. Using 1:50000 and 1:25000 scale Ordnance Survey maps:
   - interpret contour lines in terms of shape and steepness of terrain. Learn what the topographical features mean, including valley, col, ridge and spur.

- show how to set a map, with and without a compass. Learn how to use and give six-figure grid references. Demonstrate the use of a roamer to improve accuracy.
  - show how to find north without the aid of a compass, by day or night.
3. Walk two compass routes of at least 5 kilometres each. They should be defined on a map, one route's start and end points defined by you and the other by an adult.
4. Show you know how to dress appropriately for the walk and what kit you and your group need.
5. Choose the most appropriate type of map for the journey you are taking.

Navigator – stage 5
How to earn your badge
1. Using a 1:25000 scale Ordnance Survey map and compass, navigate along a course of at least six 'legs' to the standard of the Hill and Moorland Leader award provided by Mountain Training. This replaces the Walking Group Leader Award. You're not expected to hold this award – just have a look at the course to get an idea of the level you need to achieve. Find out more at mountain-training.org
2. Using only a compass and pacing, successfully navigate a course of at least four 'legs'.

3. Using only a map, successfully navigate a course of at least four 'legs'.
4. Make two sketch maps – one of an urban and one of a rural setting – that would enable a stranger to travel successfully between two points.
5. Complete at least three different orienteering courses in a reasonable time.
6. Complete a comprehensive route plan for a 20km hill walking route, set by an appropriate adult. It should take place in terrain one or terrain two, details of which can be found in Policy Organisation and Rules.
7. Show you know what the most appropriate clothing and equipment is for your journey.

NIGHTS AWAY

Setting off on an overnight
expedition gives you a real feeling
of freedom. These staged badges
recognise your experience and ability
to go on nights away, safely and responsibly.

How to earn your badges
You can pick up badges for having taken the
following numbers of nights away:

1	2	3	4	5	10	15	20
35	50	75	100	125	150	175	200

These are for recognised Scout activities, sleeping
in tents, bivouacs, hostels, on boats or at
other centres.

You must be properly equipped for your
activity and the weather conditions.

PADDLE SPORTS

Paddle sports are a fantastic, fun way to explore rivers, canals and lakes. You can build on your skills in either a canoe or a kayak, working with other people if you need to.

Paddle Sports – stage 1
How to earn your badge

1. Identify different types of paddle craft.
2. Name three places you could safely go canoeing or kayaking.
3. Take part in a warm up activity to prepare you for canoeing or kayaking. You could practice balancing whilst kneeling, getting in and out of a boat or practicing a paddling action.
4. Dress properly for your chosen activity. Show you know the importance of buoyancy aids and how to put one on correctly.
5. Take part in a taster session that covers:
   - naming equipment used and the parts of the boat
   - getting into and out of a boat safely
   - balancing a boat
   - manoeuvring your boat in different directions, including moving forward.

If you have achieved the British Canoeing's Paddle Power Start you can automatically gain this badge.

Top tips
You can complete most of these steps without actually being on the water, although it's best to complete them as part of a practical paddle sports activity.

Your leader will find lots of activities in Programmes Online as well as on the British Canoe Union website. Visit **canoe-england.org.uk/youth/information-for-clubs-and-coaches-/scouting**

Paddle Sports – stage 2
How to earn your badge
Before you attempt Stage 2, you need to have completed all the steps for Paddle Sports Stage 1. You then need to complete all the tasks outlined.
1. Lift, carry and launch a boat.
2. Paddle forward in a straight line.
3. Show you can steer around a course.
4. Show you can stop the boat safely.
5. Show you can exit the boat onto the shore safely.
6. Capsize, swim to the shore and empty the boat of water.

If you have achieved the British Canoeing's Paddle Power Passport you can automatically gain this badge.

Paddle Sports – stage 3
How to earn your badge

Before you attempt Stage 3, you need to have completed all the steps for Paddle Sports Stage 2. You then need to complete all the tasks outlined, using a different boat to Stage 2.

1. With help, show more than one safe method for lifting and carrying your boat.
2. Demonstrate two different ways of safely launching your boat.
3. Show you can get in and out of your boat without help.
4. Paddle forwards and backwards in a straight line, keeping good posture.
5. Show you can steer around a figure of eight course.
6. Show you can stop the boat safely when it's moving back and forth.
7. Capsize, swim to the shore and empty the boat of water.
8. Assist someone else back into their boat following a capsize.

If you have achieved the British Canoeing's Paddle Power Discover you can automatically gain this badge.

Paddle Sports – stage 4
How to earn your badge
Before you attempt Stage 4, you need to have completed all the steps for Paddle Sports Stage 3. You then need to complete all the tasks outlined.

1. Choose two of the disciplines below and paddle your boat for at least 200m in each discipline:
   - crew. Choose from K2 (two man kayak), K4 (four man kayak), C2 (two man canoe) or OC2 (two man canoe with outrigger).
   - flat wate
   - white water
   - touring
   - short boat
   - ergo.
2. Take part in at least two of the following activities that you have not tried before:
   - freestyle
   - marathon
   - polo
   - slalom
   - sprint
   - surf
   - time trial
   - wild water.

If you have achieved the British Canoeing's Paddle Power Explore Level 7 you can automatically gain this badge.

SAILING

Build up the skills to explore the seas as you work your way through these staged sailing badges.

Sailing – stage 1
How to earn your badge

1. Identify different types of sailing crafts.
2. Name three places you could safely go sailing.
3. Take part in a warm up activity to prepare you for a sailing activity. You could try tacking and gybing, hiking out or syncro-jump to cross the boat together in a tack or gybe. Your leader will find ideas for this step in Programmes Online.
4. Dress properly for a sailing activity, showing you know the importance of buoyancy aids and how to put one on correctly.
5. Take part in a taster session that covers:
   - being able to name equipment used and parts of the boat
   - getting into and out of a boat safely
   - balancing a boat
   - manoeuvring your boat in different directions, including moving forward.

You can complete most of these steps without actually being on the water, although it's best to complete them as part of a sailing activity.

If you have achieved the RYA Youth Sailing Scheme Stage 1 you can automatically gain this badge.

Sailing – stage 2
How to earn your badge
Before you attempt Stage 2, you need to have completed all the steps for Sailing Stage 1. You then need to complete all the tasks outlined.

1. Launch and recover your dinghy.
2. Control the direction and speed of your dinghy to steer around a course.
3. Stop your dinghy safely.
4. Capsize and get to the shore safely and recover the dinghy.
5. Show you can moor your dinghy.

If you have achieved the RYA Youth Sailing Scheme Stage 2 you can automatically gain this badge.

Sailing – stage 3
How to earn your badge
Before you attempt Stage 3, you need to have completed all the steps for Sailing Stage 2. You then need to complete all the tasks outlined, ideally in a different boat to Stage 2.

If you're using a keelboat, you don't have to complete steps 1-3.

1. Prepare, launch and recover your boat in an onshore wind.
2. Show the correct way to store your boat ashore.
3. Show you can right a capsized dinghy as helm or crew.
4. Show you know how to recover a man overboard.
5. Demonstrate an ability in:
   - sail setting
   - balance
   - trim
   - course made good
   - centreboard
   - taking upwind
   - gybing from a training run
   - coming alongside a moored boat
   - picking up a mooring.
6. Learn how a sail works and its basic aerodynamics.
7. When sailing, show you can understand and use basic terminology, such as windward, leeward, and bear away.

If you have achieved The Scout Association Personal Activity Permit for Dinghy Sailing or hold the RYA Youth Sailing Scheme Stage 3 you can automatically gain this badge.

Sailing – stage 4
How to earn your badge
1. Launch and recover your boat in any wind direction.
2. Set up your boat according to weather conditions, using sail and rig controls.
3. Show that you're able to recover a man overboard.
4. Show that you know about:
   - International Regulations for Preventing Collision at Sea (IRPCS)
   - Beaufort Scale
   - synoptic charts
   - tidal ebb and flow
   - spring and neap tides.

If you hold the RYA Youth Sailing Scheme Stage 4 you can automatically gain this badge.

SNOWSPORTS

Regardless of whether you're a beginner, or an experienced snowboarder or skier, this badge will improve your skills and teach you all you need to know to safely enjoy the snow.

Snowsports – stage 1
How to earn your badge

1. Identify different types of snowsports.
2. Name three places you could safely take part in snowsport activities.
3. Take part in a warm up activity to prepare you for a snowsport activity such as skiing or snowboarding. This should be an appropriate warm up for your upper, middle and lower body.
4. Dress properly for your chosen activity. Show you know the importance of helmets and how to put one on correctly.
5. Take part in a taster session that covers:
   - naming equipment used
   - how to get in and out of your skis or snowboard
   - balancing on your skis or snowboard
   - moving around on your skis or snowboard; including moving in a straight line, controlling your speed and stopping.

Top tips
You can do most of these steps without actually taking part in a snowsport activity on either a natural or artificial slope. But we think it's best to do them as part of a practical activity.

Your leader should be able to find lots of support on the National Governing Body websites for Snowsport England, Snowsport Scotland and Snowsport Cymru Wales.

More support for disability snowsports can be found on the Disability Snowsport UK website.

Snowsports – stage 2
How to earn your badge
Before you attempt Stage 2, you need to have completed all the steps for Snowsports
Stage 1. You then need to complete all the steps outlined below.

1. Identify the equipment you require and know how to carry it safely.
2. Climb and then ski or snowboard down a short run, or go on a short cross country ski.
3. Show you can make wide and narrow turns.
4. Show you can stop and wait safely on a run avoiding other users of the slope, or stop safely if doing cross country skiing.

5. Demonstrate how to safely use a drag lift or magic carpet for downhill skiing or snowboarding.
6. Know how to safely fall and get back up onto your feet.

Top tips
You can do most of these steps on either a natural or artificial slope. This badge can be completed doing cross country skiing as the activity, in which case element 5 should be replaced with the ability to identify a suitable route.

Your leader should be able to find lots of support on the National Governing Body websites for Snowsport England, Snowsport Scotland and Snowsport Cymru Wales.

More support for disability snowsports can be found on the Disability Snowsport UK website.

Snowsports – stage 3
How to earn your badge
Before you attempt Stage 3, you need to have completed all the steps for Snowsports Stage 2. You then need to complete the following:

1. Identify hazards of the mountain environment.
2. Show you understand what to do in the event of an accident.

3. Show you know and understand the 'Ski Way Code' published by the International Ski Federation (The F.I.S.)
4. Understand the effects of extreme temperature in cases of frostbite, hypothermia, sunstroke, heat exhaustion and dehydration. Explain how they are avoided and treated.
5. Choose and complete two of the following:
   - Demonstrate a sequence of 10 linked turns
   - Complete a free run down a moderate to hard slope (red) showing balance, control, good choice of line and awareness of other people on the slope
   - Complete a 3km cross country ski route on a prepared track
   - Complete a 500m cross country ski route on varied terrain

If you have achieved The Scout Association Personal Activity Permit for Snowsports, you can automatically gain this badge.
The safety rules in chapter nine of Policy Organisation and Rules and the Adventurous Activity Permit Scheme apply when you're attempting this badge.

Snowsports – stage 4
How to earn your badge

Before you attempt Stage 4, you need to have completed all the requirements to gain Snowsports Stage 3 in your chosen discipline. You then need to complete the following:

1. Show you understand what equipment to carry for the different two types of activity you may undertake (a single lesson, day on the hill, expedition in the woods, off-piste experience, session at a snow park)
2. Show how to look after yourself and others in the event of not being able to return down the mountain, or being stranded on a route
3. Show your ability to use a ski map or resort map and identify where you are on the map
4. Plan a half days activity, considering location, group, equipment and abilities, this should include a plan B in case of bad weather, etc.
5. Participate in a snowsport activity different from that which the other requirements have been completed in, this could be something completely new or an activity you've not done for a while such as skiing, snowboarding, cross country skiing, ski touring and slalom
6. Choose and complete two of the following:
   • Demonstrate your ability to safely descend a black run

- Perform a sequence of turns in fresh snow, leaving even tracks behind
- Complete a day's cross country ski trip, planning your route before you go
- Complete a cross country timed route and then improve your time over a two further attempts

You can do this stage by taking part in a snowsport activity on either a natural or artificial slope. But it is encouraged to experience both environments as part of this badge.

SWIMMER

With plenty of practice and a little confidence, you can learn to cut through the water effortlessly and with an expert stroke.

Swimmer – stage 1
How to earn your badge
1. Learn the general safety rules for swimming (such as not diving into shallow water or not swimming on your own) and where it is safe to swim locally.
2. Show you know how to prepare for exercises such as taking part in a warm up.

3. Demonstrate a controlled entry, without using the steps, into at least 1.5 metres of water.
4. Swim 10 metres on your front.
5. Tread water for 30 seconds in a vertical position.
6. Using a buoyancy aid, float still in the water for 30 seconds.
7. Demonstrate your ability to retrieve an object from chest-deep water.
8. Perform a push and glide on both your front and back.
9. Swim 25 metres without stopping.
10. Take part in an organised swimming activity.

Swimmer – stage 2
How to earn your badge
1. Learn the general safety rules for swimming (such as not diving into shallow water or not swimming on your own) and where it is safe to swim locally.
2. Show you know how to prepare for exercises such as taking part in a warm up.
3. Demonstrate a controlled entry or dive from the side of the pool, into at least 1.5 metres of water.
4. Swim 10 metres on your front, 10 metres on your back and 10 metres on your back using only your legs.
5. Tread water for three minutes in a vertical position.

6. Surface dive into at least 1.5 metres of water and touch the bottom with both hands.
7. Mushroom float for ten seconds.
8. Enter the pool and push off from the side on your front, gliding for five metres.
9. From the side of the pool, push off on your back and glide for as far as possible.
10. Swim 100 metres without stopping.
11. Take part in an organised swimming activity.

Swimmer – stage 3
How to earn your badge
1. Learn the general safety rules for swimming (such as not diving into shallow water or not swimming on your own) and where it is safe to swim locally.
2. Show you know how to prepare for exercises. You could do this by leading a warm up.
3. Demonstrate a controlled entry or dive from the side of the pool into at least 1.5 metres of water.
4. Swim 50 metres in shirt and shorts.
5. Tread water for three minutes, with one hand behind your back.
6. Surface dive into 1.5 metres of water and recover an object with both hands from the bottom. Return to the side of the pool, holding the object in both hands.

7. Enter the water from the side of the pool by sliding in from a sitting position. Using any floating object for support, take up and hold the heat escape lessening posture for five minutes.
8. Swim 400 metres without stopping.
9. Take part in a different organised swimming activity to the one on your previous swimming badge.

Swimmer – stage 4
How to earn your badge
1. Learn the general safety rules for swimming (such as not diving into shallow water or not swimming on your own) and where it is safe to swim locally.
2. Show you know how to prepare for exercises. You could do this by leading a warm up.
3. Demonstrate a racing dive into at least 1.8 metres of water and straddle jump into at least 2 meters of water.
4. Swim 100 metres in less than four minutes.
5. Tread water for five minutes.
6. Surface dive into 1.5 metres of water, both head first and feet first and swim at least 5 metres under water on both occasions.
7. Enter the water as you would if you didn't know the depth. Swim 10 metres to a floating object. Use the object to take up and hold the heat escape lessening posture for five minutes.

8. Swim 800 metres using any of the four recognised strokes without stopping. You should swim 400m on your front and 400m on your back.
9. Take part in an organised swimming activity that's different to the one on your previous swimming badge.

Swimmer – stage 5
How to earn your badge
1. Learn the general safety rules for swimming (such as not diving into shallow water or not swimming on your own) and where it is safe to swim locally.
2. Show you know how to prepare for exercises. You could do this by leading a warm up.
3. Demonstrate a racing dive into at least 1.8 metres of water and a straddle jump into at least 2 meters of water.
4. Swim 100 metres in shirt and shorts. When you've finished, remove the shirt and shorts and climb out of the pool unaided. Your time limit is three minutes.
5. Tread water for five minutes, three of which one arm must be held clear of the water.
6. Scull on your back, head first, for ten metres, then feet first for ten metres. Move into a tuck position and turn 360 degrees, keeping your head out of the water.

7. Swim 10 metres, perform a somersault without touching the side of the pool, then carry on swimming in the same direction for a further 10 metres.

8. Demonstrate the heat escape lessening posture.

9. Demonstrate a surface dive, both head and feet first, into 1.5 metres of water.

10. Swim 1,000 metres using any of the four recognised strokes, for a minimum distance of 200 metres per stroke. This swim must be completed in 35 minutes.

11. Take part in an organised swimming activity that's different to the one on your previous swimming badge.

TIME ON THE WATER

If you're building up your experience in boating or water sport activities, you can gain badges to recognise your achievement as you go.

You can collect Time on the Water staged badges when you take part in any of these activities, as long as each session lasts about 2-3 hours:

- kayaking
- canoeing
- sailing
- windsurfing
- powerboating
- kiteboarding
- surfing
- yachting
- motorcruising
- narrowboating
- pulling or rowing
- paddleboarding
- white water rafting
- traditional rafting.

And as you complete the following number of activities, you can gain a badge:

1   2   5   10   15   20   35   50

You must be properly dressed and equipped for your activity and the weather conditions. Your leader will also need to make sure you're following the activity rules in chapter nine of the Policy and Organisation Rules and the Activity Permit Scheme.

CHALLENGE AWARDS

BE THE BEST YOU CAN BE...

Awards

Badges aren't the only way you can be rewarded in Scouts. You can earn awards as you go through Scouts and take part in special challenges. They all help to make your time in Scouts fun, interesting and worthwhile. And as you earn them, you can work towards the big one – the Chief Scout's Gold Award.

Challenge Awards

There are nine awards in the Scouts section. They're different to the other badges because you'll do these with other Scouts, rather than outside of meetings or at home.

ADVENTURE CHALLENGE AWARD

How to earn your award

1. Take part in four different adventurous activities. At least two of these activities should be new to you and you should try to do them on at least two separate occasions.

   You could try:
   - abseiling
   - canoeing
   - caving or potholing
   - climbing
   - cycling
   - dragon boating
   - gliding
   - hill walking
   - hiking
   - hovercrafting
   - mountain boarding
   - night hiking
   - orienteering
   - paragliding
   - pony trekking or horse riding
   - powered aircraft
   - pulling
   - rafting
   - sailing

- snowboarding
- stunt kiting
- sub-aqua
- surfing
- water-skiing
- windsurfing.

2. Show how you have developed your skill and expertise in one of these activities. Show that you know the safety issues involved, and that you can use any equipment needed for the activity safely.

3. Learn about any environmental issues caused by your activity. Take steps to reduce any harm to the environment.

4. Research other ways you can take part, or develop your skills, in your chosen activities. Follow up your research with action!

Top tips

You can take part in other activities, not just the ones we've suggested, so long as it's adventurous. Visit **scouts.org.uk/a-z** for more ideas.

 The safety rules for all activities can be found at **scouts.org.uk/a-z**

CHALLENGE AWARDS

CREATIVE CHALLENGE AWARD

How to earn your award

1. Over a period of time, take part in at least four creative activities. Some of these should be new to you.
   You could try:
   - music
   - photography
   - wood or metalwork
   - needlework
   - cooking
   - website design
   - dance.
2. Show that you have developed your skills in one of these activities. Show that you know how to use any equipment safely.
3. Use your creative ability to produce something that promotes a Scouting activity or an event.
4. Construct a model using materials like a plastic kit or recycled items. Alternatively, make a useful item from wood, metal or plastic.
5. Show how to use social media or the internet in a creative and safe way. Explain why it's important to use them safely.

6. Take part in a performance.
   You could try:
   - magic tricks
   - gymnastics display
   - campfire sketch
   - street dance
   - plays
   - concerts.

EXPEDITION CHALLENGE AWARD

How to earn your award

1. Take part in either an expedition or an exploration over two days with at least three other Scouts. This should include a night away at a campsite or hostel.

2. Take an active part in planning the expedition. Do any training you need and be well prepared. Training should include:
   - planning a route, including rest and meal stops. Being able to work out how long it should take you to travel that route.
   - choosing suitable equipment for an expedition. You might consider tents, stoves, rucksacks, walking equipment, emergency equipment, first aid kit, wet weather gear, appropriate food and a camera.
   - navigation and using things like maps and timetables for your expedition. You might want to brush up on using an Ordnance Survey or similar map, a compass, a GPS device, a street map or A-Z, and rail or bus timetables.
   - knowing what to do in an emergency.

3. During the expedition or exploration:
   - play a full part in the team
   - use a map or other navigation device to keep track of where you are
   - cook and eat at least one hot meal
   - do a task, investigation or exploration as agreed with your leader.
4. Produce an individual report or presentation within the three weeks following your expedition. You could present your work as a project, performance, video recording, oral presentation, blog or website.

❗ You must always follow the Nights Away and activity rules – visit **scouts.org.uk/a-z** and **scouts.org.uk/nightsaway**

Top tips
You can do an expedition by foot, cycle, canoe, horse or another acceptable means of transport, travelling for at least four hours on each day. A task or small project should be completed while you're on the journey.
You might try:
   - exploring a country or suburban area new to you
   - walking in a country park or on footpaths through woods and fields
   - walking a tow-path along a river or canal
   - a cycle ride

- canoeing or kayaking on rivers or canals
- walking part of a long distance footpath near to you

You can do an exploration by foot, cycle, public transport or another agreed mode of transport. It must take at least 90 minutes to reach the destination. Carry out at least five hours of investigation over the two days and follow up on research you've carried out.
You might try exploring:

- nature – wildlife, city farms, flowers, trees, birds, mammals, animal sanctuaries
- buildings – cathedrals, theatres, churches, mosques, temples, farms, villages, houses, cinemas
- culture/society – ghosts, legends, famous people, art galleries, sports arenas
- environment – recycling plants, nature reserves, litter, pollution, national parks, gardens
- history – prehistoric standing stones, stone circles, historic buildings, burial grounds, battle grounds, museums
- science – science museums, planetariums, power stations, switch boards, old operating theatres, medical tours, zoological collections, zoos.

Both options include a night away, which could be at a campsite, bunk house, hostel or similar.

OUTDOOR CHALLENGE AWARD

How to earn your award

1. Take an active part in at least eight nights away as a Scout. Four of the nights should be camping. While you're away, work with other Scouts do the other tasks on this list.
2. With others, pitch and strike your tent.
3. Lead, or help to lead, a group of Scouts to set up a well-organised site. It should include sleeping tents, food and equipment stores, a fire or stove, kitchen and eating area.
4. Prepare and light an open fire or set up a suitable stove. Use it to prepare, cook and serve a meal safely.
5. Understand the three points of the Countryside Code. Show what action you can take to follow the code.
6. Find out why personal and campsite hygiene is important. What should you do to be hygienic?
7. Using knots that you have learned, build a simple pioneering project, object or camp gadget.
8. Explore the environment of your camp and make sure you know where everything is. Respect the environment you are in and, at the end of the camp, leave the site as you found it.

9. Find out what accidents and incidents can happen outdoors or during your camp. Show how you would deal with them.

10. Show how to use an axe, saw or knife safely. You can choose any or all of these tools.

11. Complete at least four of these tasks:
- Provide a service commitment to the site for about an hour.
- Take part in a wide game.
- Take part in a campfire or other entertainment.
- Working with others, successfully complete a two-hour activity or project.
- Plan a balanced menu for a short camp.
- Lead the cooking of a meal for the group.
- Show that you know the safety precautions for using lamps and stoves.
- Cook a backwoods meal with the group.
- Build a bivouac and sleep in it.
- Show how to pack a rucksack correctly, with appropriate kit for the camp or event.

Top tips

If you're not able to stay away overnight for any reason, remember your leader might be able to offer an alternative.

You must always follow the Nights Away and activity rules – **visit scouts.org.uk/a-z** and **scouts.org.uk/nightsaway**

PERSONAL CHALLENGE AWARD

How to earn your award

Complete two personal challenges that you agree
with your leader. You should choose one of the
challenges and your leader will choose the other.
The challenges must be different from the ones
you did for your Beaver and Cub Personal
Challenge Awards.

Top tips

The challenges should be things that you find
difficult, but can overcome with some effort and
commitment. They can be to do with any part of
your life. It could be home, school or Scouts.

Here are some example challenges to help you
think about what you could do. You don't have to
pick a challenge from this list – choose something
that's personal to you.

- Support a new Scout to complete their
  Membership Award
- Give up using your mobile or games console
  for a week
- Take part in an organised walk or run
  for charity

- Talk about a topic you are interested in in front of your Patrol
- Bring the right equipment to Scouts every week for a term
- Help your younger brother or sister with their school work for a term
- Learn how to communicate in basic sign language
- Do at least an hour of physical activity every day over the summer holidays
- Gain an activity permit
- Do the washing up at home for two weeks
- Plan and run a base or activity at camp
- Organise a small fundraising event for the Group or a local charity

SKILLS CHALLENGE AWARD

How to earn your award

1. Regularly take part in physical activities over a period of four to six weeks. Keep a record showing your improvement. Your goal could be to develop in an activity or successfully complete a challenge.

Physical activity suggestions:
- circuit training
- football skill training
- aerobic routine
- synchronised swimming routine
- Zumba aerobics
- tap dancing
- team sports.

Physical challenge suggestions:
- charity swim
- long distance cycle ride
- incident hike
- athletic event
- pool life-saving test
- dance competition.

2. Show you understand why eating a sensible diet and getting enough sleep is important.

3. Do some research so that you can explain the dangers and harmful effects of smoking, alcohol and drugs.

4. Learn and use at least five of these skills:
   - Mend or customise an item of clothing.
   - Cook and serve a two-course meal, for at least four people.
   - Fix a puncture or a dropped chain on a bike.
   - Wash up after a meal, making sure everything is clean and dry.
   - Use a washing machine to wash a load of clothes.
   - Iron your uniform shirt.
   - Change a lightbulb, in a ceiling light.
   - Set a heating timer and thermostat as needed for the time of year.
   - Clean a toilet, hob or oven.
   - Do another similar home skill.

5. Take part in at least three activities that require a number of problem solving skills.

TEAM LEADER CHALLENGE AWARD

How to earn your award

To achieve this award you need to hold the
Scout Teamwork Challenge Award, and
complete these requirements over a period
of at least three months.

1. Successfully lead a Scout team at a camp or an
   all day event. You need to:
   - Look after the whole Scout Patrol/team.
   - Help individuals in your team if they need it.
   - Make sure that your team achieves the goal
     you have been set.
2. Help a new Scout to be part of the Scout Troop
   with an understanding of what is expected
   of them.
3. Help another Scout to develop a Scouting skill.
4. Represent the views of other Scouts
   (for example at a Patrol Leaders' Council
   or something similar) and report back to
   them afterwards.

TEAMWORK CHALLENGE AWARD

How to earn your award
This award should be done over a period of at least three months.

1. On at least three separate occasions, be part of a Scout team, where you work together to achieve a goal.
2. Give at least three examples of when you've been in different types of teams. Explain your role in those teams.
3. Take part in at least three teambuilding activities that you have not tried before.
4. Take an active part in at least four Troop or Patrol Forums. At each forum, express your views on at least one item being discussed.

WORLD CHALLENGE AWARD

How to earn your award

1. Choose an aspect of local community life and find out as much as you can about it. You could learn about:
   - local government
   - local history
   - different faiths and beliefs
   - types of farming/industry found locally
2. Spend a day volunteering with and finding out about a service in your local community:
   - What are their challenges?
   - Who relies on this service?
   - What positive impact could you have on this service in the future?

   Services could be homeless shelters, local nature reserves, care homes and food banks
3. Take part in an activity which reflects upon and explores your own beliefs, attitudes and values (this may or may not include religious beliefs). What values do we share as Scouts? Which Scout value means the most to you?
4. Take part in an activity that explores common beliefs and attitudes towards gender or disability in different societies. You could look at this in the context of music, sport and fashion.

5. Take an active part in an environmental project.
6. Investigate and try to make contact with Scouts in another country. Make sure you and your leader read the International Links Guidance at scouts.org.uk/intlinks
7. Take part in an activity that explores an international issue.

CHIEF SCOUT'S GOLD AWARD

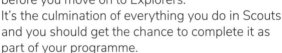

The Chief Scout's Gold Award is the highest award you can get before you move on to Explorers. It's the culmination of everything you do in Scouts and you should get the chance to complete it as part of your programme.

It'll take effort to achieve it, but it also gives you a chance to try new experiences along the way.

How to earn your award
1. Earn six activity or staged activity badges of your choice. They could be badges you gain outside of your normal meetings or ones you've achieved through your programme.
2. Complete the nine challenge awards. These are:
   - World Challenge Award
   - Skills Challenge Award

- Creative Challenge Award
- Outdoors Challenge Award
- Adventure Challenge Award
- Expedition Challenge Award
- Teamwork Challenge Award
- Team Leader Challenge Award
- Personal Challenge Award

Top tips

If you haven't quite completed the challenges for the Chief Scout's Gold Award, you can complete them in your first term in the Explorer Unit.

You can wear your Chief Scout's Silver Award on your uniform until you achieve your Chief Scout's Gold Award.

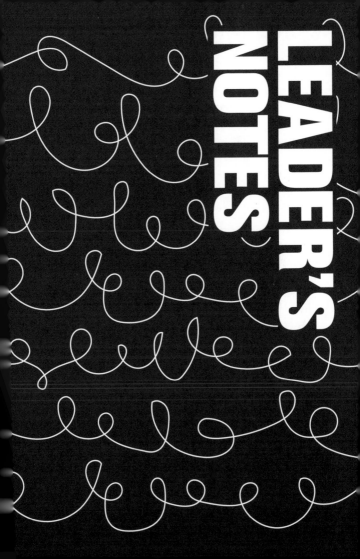

LEADER'S
NOTES

BE SUPPORTIVE...

**Notes for leaders and other adults
supporting Scouts**
This section is useful for any adult helping a Scout
to work towards their badges. You might be a
teacher, parent, carer or coach – everyone can
play a role in helping Scouts achieve their goals.

Scout badges

Badges and awards are an important part of the Scout Programme. They provide a vast array of activities that enrich Scouts' experiences and they're a great way of rewarding them. You'll probably notice that the challenges aren't easy. But in our experience Scouts enjoy working towards challenges. They're more likely to be motivated by achieving badges that take effort to complete.

Achieving and awarding badges

You don't need a formal 'assessor' to sign off that a Scout has completed a badge. Any relevant adult can confirm that the Scout has completed the requirement, such as an instructor, swimming coach, teacher or adult with knowledge of the subject. Leaders can then award the badge. You might want to encourage Scouts to bring in things that they have done to achieve their badge, such as food they have cooked, or pictures of them doing a particular activity. If Leaders talk to Scouts about what they did, they can then make an informed decision about whether the Scout has done what's required to award the badge.

When to award badges

Once a Scout has achieved all that's required for a badge, leaders should award it as soon as possible. It keeps the achievement fresh in Scouts' minds.

Most badges should be awarded at the end of a Troop meeting, but you may want to think about awarding some at a time and place that's special to the Scout. You could award a Nights Away badge while camping, or you could hold a special party for Scouts when they achieve their Chief Scout's Gold Award.

Leaders can buy badges from Scout Store at shop. scouts.org.uk

Safety for leaders

Scouting should be delivered in a safe environment and some badges include activities that involve specific safety rules or guidance. We've added an icon, like the one above, to certain badges in this book. It highlights that there are specific safety rules to follow.

For more information about safety please visit **scouts.org.uk/safety.**

For rules and guidance on organising adventurous and outdoor activities visit **scouts.org.uk/a-z**

Encouraging community impact
What is Community Impact?

The Community Impact badge encourages Scouts to take practical action in the service of others, in order to create positive social change. It benefits the wider community as well as the young people taking part. Encourage Scouts to go for this badge and help them consider these questions:

1. Do you want to take action on issues affecting people in your local area, across the country or all across the world?
2. Is the action you want to take relevant to the community you're trying to help? Or is it trying to fix a problem that doesn't exist?
3. Will it genuinely change the lives of others, or is it just a nice thing to do?
4. Will the action you want to take genuinely develop you as a person? Or is it actually quite boring, mundane and not very much fun?

Identifying need

Social issues can affect different people in different ways. Young people will face different problems from older people. Those living in the countryside will have different challenges from those who live in a city centre. Social issues in Scotland are very different from those in Tibet.

This requirement is about knowing what issues are relevant to the people you are trying to help. Young people should ask themselves:

1. Who in our chosen community will be an expert in the issues and challenges people face or are passionate about?
2. Are there other sources of research or information we can use to identify issues?
3. What issues do we care about?

Planning action

Community impact is about creating positive social change, so Scouts must be clear on what exactly they want to change before deciding on what practical action to take. You should help young people to ask themselves, in this order:

1. What is the problem they are trying to fix?
2. What needs to change to fix that problem?
3. What can we actually do to make that change?

Learning and continuing to make change

Community impact should develop the young person taking part, so your projects should have some kind of learning outcome. Young people should be given space to reflect and talk about what they have learned.

1. What have they learned about the issue they took action on?
2. What skills have they learned?
3. How have their values and attitudes developed?

The project should also contribute to social change, and that is unlikely to happen in a short space of time. So once they reach a stage where they consider their project finished, you should support young people to think further.

1. How could they improve their Community Impact project so that it reaches more people and makes a bigger impact?
2. How could they involve more people in their project?
3. Would they consider participating in a community impact project run by another organisation or group on the same or different issues?

Celebrating the work and inspiring others

Social change happens when others are inspired to take action. You should support young people to reach and inspire more people who can take action on their chosen issue. You could do this through:

- interacting with local media
- presenting to relevant groups of people such as local business, decision makers and other community groups
- interacting with other non-Scouting youth groups, such as schools, youth clubs and sports teams
- speaking to their own families, other Scout groups and sections.

For resources to support community impact, visit the A Million Hands website at **amillionhands.org.uk**

Staying safe online

Digital Citizen and Digital Maker staged activity badges may involve performing some tasks online, and finding out about social networking. Before Scouts take part in these activities, you'll want to talk through a few safety rules first.

Check that Scouts understand that staying safe involves:

- knowing what makes a good secure password, how to protect your password, and how a password manager could help with this
- knowing why it might not be safe to log in to websites using other accounts like Facebook or Twitter, as this increases vulnerability of data sharing across software
- spotting fake anti-virus software and updates
- understanding what kind of websites have privacy policies and why, how they can look for privacy policies and seals of approval, and which information they should avoid sharing online because it's private
- understanding who owns information, what plagiarism is, and how giving credit is a sign of respect for other people's work
- understanding that some websites don't contain the truth, and being able to investigate or follow up on sources to decide reliability

- telling the difference between online friends and real life, face-to-face friends, and how they might communicate differently with them.
- protecting their social networking profile and online image. They need to think carefully about their username, pictures and what they share.
- understanding what cyberbullying is, ways to deal with it, and what they can do when it happens
- understanding that the purpose of online advertising is to make people want to buy products, and that online ads often target them.

Social networking

Examples of social networking sites that are suitable for the Scout (10-14) age group include:

- Kibooku (6-13)
- Moshi Monsters (6-12)
- YourSphere (6-17)
- Skooville (6-14)
- ScuttlePad (6-11)
- SuperClubsPLUS (6-12)
- Club Penguin (6-14).

Remember that for some social networking sites Scouts must be aged 13 or over, including: Facebook, Flickr, Google+.

You can find useful information and resources to help you talk about online safety with young people at:

- NSPCC website at **nspcc.org.uk/onlinesafety**
- CEOP's online safety site **thinkuknow.co.uk**
- Digizen, digital awareness site **digizen.org**
- Childnet's 'Know it all online' safety advice **childnet.com/resources/kia**

Adapting Badge and Award Requirements

Each young person who participates in the Programme, including badges and awards, should face a similar degree of challenge, and requirements can be adapted according to each young person's abilities.

The guiding principle throughout the Programme should be that young people are being challenged, while having fun. The requirements for badges provide a wide range of choice for young people, and most will be able to access the badges of their choice.

You may need to adjust the challenge to ensure that young people of different abilities all experience a similar level of challenge.

Adaptations made for young people with additional needs, medical conditions or disabilities should be aimed at improving access to the badge rather than reducing the challenge of its requirements or changing the focus. This may involve adapting some or all of the requirements and/or providing appropriate additional support.

In some instances, it may be appropriate to support the young people in your section to understand the adjustments, explaining that being fair doesn't always mean everyone doing exactly the same thing. In this situation, fair is about everyone being able to access the activity and experience a similar level of challenge. The nature of your conversation should take into consideration the age of the young people involved, the specific circumstances and the adaptations being made.

It is entirely up to the Leader how to adapt some or all of the badge or award requirements, in consultation with the young person and their parents or carers.

The things to consider are:

1. Whether the individual requirements can be adapted or whether they need to be replaced by an entirely different activity.
2. Whether to change the requirements for one young person or whether it is more appropriate to change them for the whole section to ensure the young person doesn't feel singled out.
3. Adapting some of the individual challenges into a team challenge, so that the young person can use their individual strengths and abilities to achieve a team goal. Again, this avoids one Member being singled out.
4. When a badge or award is being undertaken as part of a group activity, it may be appropriate for all of the young people to be involved in the decision to alter the requirements. This will support the young people to better understand the reasons for the changes and be able to offer peer support.

For more information and tips about supporting young people with additional needs to fully participate in Scouting, see the Scouting for All section on the members area of scouts.org.uk

For further support please contact info.centre@scouts.org.uk

SCOUT UNIFORM

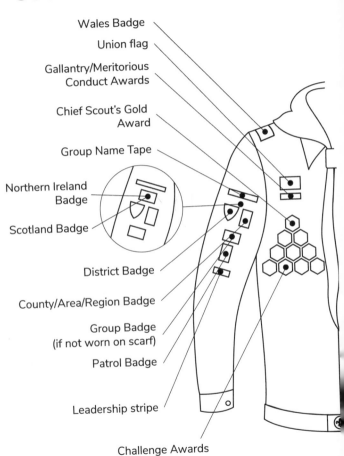

Wales Badge

Union flag

Gallantry/Meritorious Conduct Awards

Chief Scout's Gold Award

Group Name Tape

Northern Ireland Badge

Scotland Badge

District Badge

County/Area/Region Badge

Group Badge (if not worn on scarf)

Patrol Badge

Leadership stripe

Challenge Awards

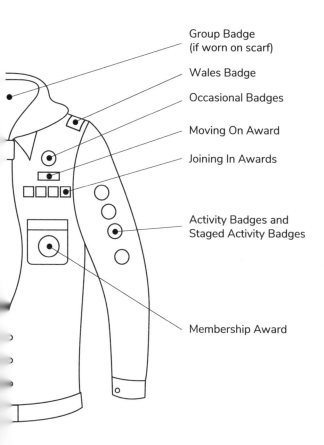

Group Badge
(if worn on scarf)

Wales Badge

Occasional Badges

Moving On Award

Joining In Awards

Activity Badges and
Staged Activity Badges

Membership Award

SCOUT JUMPER (SEA)

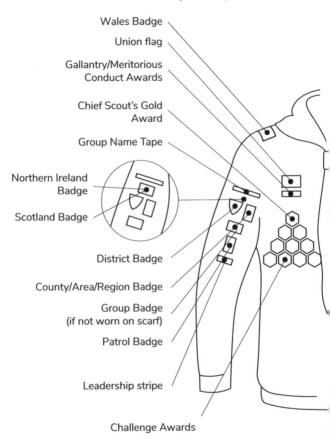

Wales Badge

Union flag

Gallantry/Meritorious Conduct Awards

Chief Scout's Gold Award

Group Name Tape

Northern Ireland Badge

Scotland Badge

District Badge

County/Area/Region Badge

Group Badge (if not worn on scarf)

Patrol Badge

Leadership stripe

Challenge Awards

*Only Royal Navy (RN) Recognised
Royal Navy Scouts are permitted to wear the RN
Recognition Badge.

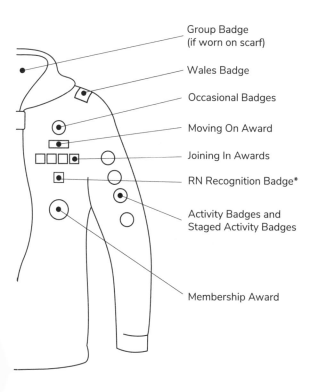

Group Badge
(if worn on scarf)

Wales Badge

Occasional Badges

Moving On Award

Joining In Awards

RN Recognition Badge*

Activity Badges and
Staged Activity Badges

Membership Award

SCOUT UNIFORM (AIR)

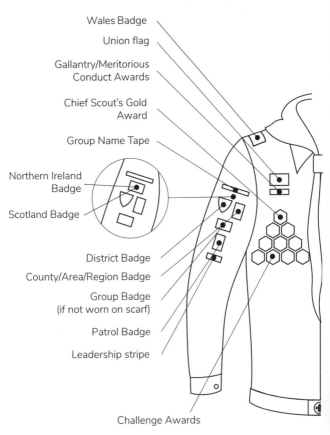

Wales Badge

Union flag

Gallantry/Meritorious
Conduct Awards

Chief Scout's Gold
Award

Group Name Tape

Northern Ireland
Badge

Scotland Badge

District Badge

County/Area/Region Badge

Group Badge
(if not worn on scarf)

Patrol Badge

Leadership stripe

Challenge Awards

*Only Royal Air Force (RAF) Recognised Air Scouts are permitted to wear the RAF Recognition Badge.

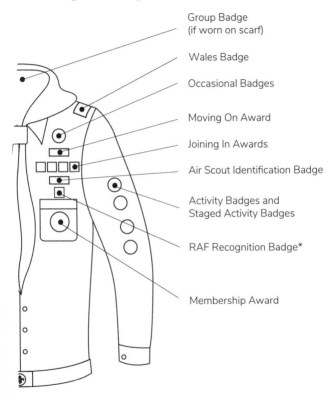

Group Badge
(if worn on scarf)

Wales Badge

Occasional Badges

Moving On Award

Joining In Awards

Air Scout Identification Badge

Activity Badges and
Staged Activity Badges

RAF Recognition Badge*

Membership Award

SCOUT UNIFORM (SEA)

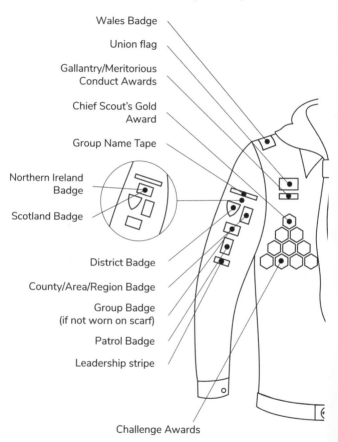

Wales Badge

Union flag

Gallantry/Meritorious Conduct Awards

Chief Scout's Gold Award

Group Name Tape

Northern Ireland Badge

Scotland Badge

District Badge

County/Area/Region Badge

Group Badge (if not worn on scarf)

Patrol Badge

Leadership stripe

Challenge Awards

*Only Royal Navy (RN) Recognised
Royal Navy Scouts are permitted to wear the RN
Recognition Badge.

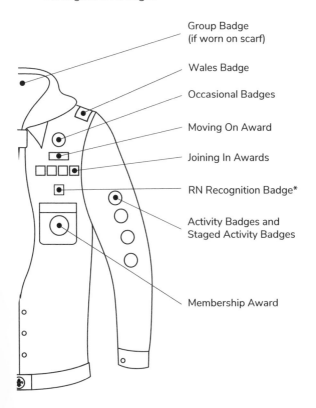

Group Badge
(if worn on scarf)

Wales Badge

Occasional Badges

Moving On Award

Joining In Awards

RN Recognition Badge*

Activity Badges and
Staged Activity Badges

Membership Award

NOTES

NOTES

NOTES

NOTES

NOTES